Bamboo & Fern

By

Ava Brown

New Generation **Publishing**

Dedication

To my mum Una and my children Chardonae,
Elizabeth and Mikhel Kai, with all my love.

Ava Brown was born and brought up in St Elizabeth, Jamaica. She trained as a secondary teacher at the Sam Sharpe Teachers college in Montego Bay Jamaica followed by an MBA in Business Administration at the University of Wales, United Kingdom.

Married to Boniface Uduhirinwa (Chuck), she lives in London and is the mother of two children who she calls her life. Ava currently works in Critical Infomration Handling, as well as is CEO for her consultant company Chakai Consultants Ltd. "Bamboo and Fern" is her first book from which she is set to launch "Ava's Kitchen" *A life Coach and Family Food Therapist Project*.

She is currently working on her second novel *"Walk on through your dream"*.

This book is dedicated to you guys with all my love:
Mum (Una Beckford)

Thank you mama for choosing to bring a child into the world when you were a child yourself. This could not have been an easy decision, especially when your parents put you out on the streets, so you had to grow up fast. That must have been tough. Until recently I did not understand your inability to show love emotionally or physically, but I know you love us when you know we are coming and you sacrifice the last $100 and buy a "tups" of salted fish to ensure we had food to eat. You gave us the most and remained hungry at times, you fussed over us and made us feel like princesses..............mama I love you.

My daughter Chardonae Elizabeth

Char, as a child you had to grow up so fast and see some of mum's struggles. It's my hope that they strengthen you and make you a warrior of a woman but with a heart of an angel. You have been the best daughter I could have asked for and would not change anything. I am thankful that the challenges have not broken us but made us a stronger mother daughter and most importantly friends. All my love mum xxx

My son Mikhel Kai

Mikhel you came into my life long before this was written but you are such a sweet son who has added joy daily, whether it is with your smile or just asking for a cuddle. Little did you know that you are adding to my life daily especially at times when writing, proofreading or editing a piece of Bamboo & Fern was just a difficult thing to do. Those cuddles helped, with all my love mum xxx.

Acknowledgements

My husband, *Nkem Chuck*, thanks for putting up with me. It's not been easy, but you have tenacity and resilience, but more importantly, you have loved me from the first time we met. Even through some of the most difficult times, you failed to give up on me and for that I say thanks a million love.

Auntie Norma Knight, I love you. Thanks for the love through the years and the belief in me over the years. More importantly for the gift of a trip to London that would change the direction of my story.

Jean Marie Thompson (my confidant and friend), thanks for all your support over the years. You gave me the name for my book, without even knowing, in an email you sent me through some of the tough times. You are such a caring soul, someone who took me into her arms amidst the risk. Thanks for the late night chats, the running up of your phone bills and even sending me money when I was stone broke. Jay you were my sanctuary, when I needed to off load you just sat and took it all in. I always felt better walking away after my sessions with you.

Yvonne Asafu-Adjaye thanks for being there when I got locked up and could have lost my child to social services. Thanks for standing in the gap for me and being a great friend.

Buju Leonard Brooks (my step father) the man who fed me when my own father didn't care to. Who would give me the last piece of meat on his plate and ensured that, regardless of how little, we had food. Thanks for everything.

Uncle Ken Brown. My real Daddy thanks for being my daddy, thanks for showing me how a dad should love his child..........you didn't have to, but took it on yourself.

Yvonne Miller. Thanks for being my childhood friend and now my adult friend and made me godmother of your beautiful daughter.

Babalwa Tiwali. Though in South Africa and we are apart, thanks for the support you gave in London. Girl you are my angel; you saved me many times with child care and that meant a lot.

Saffron Jackson thanks for the friendship, care and love you added to my life here in London.

Kenya Uter Morrison thanks for the support both in writing and kicking me to get on with it, but more so for the love you showed me even though I lost it sometimes with you. Your faith in God has been something that has inspired me and lead me closer to his love. I can confidently call you *friend*.

Joy Kingston you helped me feed my child by getting me work on many occasions and for that I love you, but more so you are my friend.

Cheryl Gregory, oh my love, friend, biggest cheer leader and confidant. I am so blessed to have someone like you who has guided me for years and put up with my madness when I get stressed. You are an amazing friend who I truly love. Oh how I love you, you have taken so much of my sharp tongue when frustrated and yet still love me dearly. **You are one of my rocks.**

Dario Pirjak, the stranger who believed in me and became one of my **motivators and life coach**. Your counsel, belief, wisdom and, most importantly, consistent listening ears are totally appreciated. I admire your zeal for success that's rubbing off on me.

Angels who gave me wings over the years:

The Honourable Ambassador Burchell Whiteman, you gave me my first real chance. May you continue to be a believer in young people such as myself.

Mavis Taylor, Mrs Johnson & Myki Mitchell (Former teachers St. Elizabeth Technical High School). You guys mothered me and molded the little ability I possessed at the time. *Mrs. Taylor* you fed me when I was hungry, sometimes without even knowing. I thank god for you all, three women who inspired my drive through their belief in me.

My Editors

Main Editor: *Jennifer van Velkinburgh*, Jen you have taken my gibberish and made it come alive, your creativity and ability to have found my voice was outstanding. Thanks for the personal session given when I was down. You are simply amazing.

Pre Editor : *Joanna Thompson*, babes thanks for the help you gave in putting my preamble in a better frame so that Jennifer could make head or tail from it all. I have truly appreciated all you did my love.

My publisher: *New Generation* thanks for the guidance through this entire publishing process; you have held my hands through it all. It was seamless in the end and that is service extraordinaire.

Ava x

Foreword

I do not remember all of the exact words said in all of the stressful situations I have endured, but I do remember the gist of what was said and I have attempted to the best of my abilities to recreate the extreme stress and anxiety of those situations.

Chapter 1

"Birth is a special time for any mother; she forgets all her struggles and latches unto the bundle of joy she is gifted with."

To understand the woman I am today, you'll have to first learn the story of my beginnings. I was born in an old post office in a poor district near Georges Valley, Jamaica. My mother, who was only fifteen or sixteen at the time and far too young to be a mum, was almost as much of a stranger in this district as I was, having been put out by her parents with 'good riddance' for the trouble she (and I) represented. I've been told that she had chosen this district, which adjoined her own, because this is where she thought my father was from. Of course, she had gone straight to his parent's home, which was one of the community's largest and most impressive, hoping to find shelter. Yet, when she turned up on their doorstep to say that she was pregnant with their son's child, his mother furiously chased my mum away, answering her request for support and food by mockingly suggesting that she start collecting dirt to make the Milo (a chocolaty drink that all children loved) for her bastard spawn. Shortly thereafter, the young man who was supposed to be my dad absconded. In my childish mind, I imagined him as a scared young man, fleeing the massive responsibility that was to come with a child, hoping to live out the rest of his youth in the carefree manner that all young men seem to crave. It was only as an adult, however, that I began to understand the implications of the rumours that had always circulated around me, whispers that my father's parent's response could be based on the fact that he felt I wasn't his child.

Alone and pregnant in this new town, my mother switched her efforts to finding a new boyfriend to be her breadwinner. She quickly found Jack who was employed at the nearby rice factory, and this was the familial situation into which I was born. Despite Jack making scarcely enough to feed himself, I don't remember my mother ever having a proper job. Yet, it was painfully clear to me, even as a young child, that our family was poor; by seven years-old the hunger in my belly had already ignited the flame that that was to propel me out of our one-room house, which was by then bursting at its seams to hold my step-father, mother and three siblings as well as myself. Though I had no idea of how I would escape the misery within its walls, I had a fire in my blood that would have burned that little shack down.

Inside the house, a sheet was used to separate us – the adults on one side and us four children on the other. There was never enough bed space, and someone would always wet the bed, so we often slept soaked in urine. We awoke with the sun and the daily chores awaiting us were many. There were the goats to take care of, fetching the water from the only pipe that served our entire community and carrying it home, collecting wood for the fire, and washing clothes. Sometimes, we even had to cook. Babysitting was something I was expected to do from an early age. We were expected to clean the floor of our room every day, using a red dye called 'red oak', which made the concrete floor a deep red, then to polish it to a high shine. We weren't allowed to stop until my mother could see her reflection glaring up at her from below.

It always seemed to be my duty to clean our side of the room, but I had to let my frustrations at this unfairness bubble inside of me in silence, as if I didn't, a stone, machete or any solid item within my mum's reach would come towards me, flung from my mother's strong arm. I must have been born with a streak of rebellion and mother was keenly aware of this and was always ready to squash it out of me. I recall one night when I refused to complete all my chores and my mother showed me who was boss by ensuring I stayed outside for a good few hours in the pitch dark. I had been overly tired from the day when I had refused to finish my chores, instead moving my weary feet along with my siblings headed inside. But, this rebellion had not escaped my mother's attention, and she had already come up with her own plans that were unbeknownst to me – but not for long! I was at the end of the line filing in the door. When everyone else had made it inside, my mother rapidly slammed the door shut in my face and locked it. She answered my surprised cries by jerking it open again and saying, "You want to come in? Then come in nuh." Of course, I thought she was serious and I immediately moved into the doorway. Her strong grip, as she grabbed me and gave me a good hiding left me in such shock that I was more startled to find myself being pushed right back outside and the sound of the lock shutting me out being her final punishment. This had been my first taste of my mother's penalty meted on those who dared to disobey her. The darkness around me seemed darker than ever; my only light was the inconsistent flickering of the Peanie Wallies. The realisation that I was alone, left to the elements, filled my heart with a wild fear. All the ghost stories we had just told came rushing back. I could feel each dead person we had spoken about now floating around me. I crouched into a tight ball, the night's silence nearly smothering me. It was over two hours later that my brother opened the door to let me in. This was no heroic or chivalrous effort on my brother's part; my mum had allowed this kindness, I guess because she knew I had learnt my lesson. My mum told me a story of when she taught me a lesson as a child; she stated that I refused to hold one of my siblings so that she could perform in a concert. She said she got mad and tore off all my clothes from the concert venue to our house. She had a very volatile temper which scarred one of my sisters for life. My sister had gone to the shop on an errand for my mom, when she didn't come back on time mum went in search of her; upon finding her in a boy's home, she bit flesh from my sister's shoulder, scarring her for life.

The rule in our house was that children rose out of bed in the morning, were set to work and then rushed outside, forbidden to go back into the house until the sun was setting and we were ready to sleep. If we lingered in the morning, we would be awakened by a face full of cold water. However, this was rare as the bed was normally so full of people that we were already being jostled awake or pushed out by the smell and feel of urine. Before we came in the evenings, we would have to fill up pans with water for the next morning and was ourselves. Our house didn't have a bathroom, so everyone bathed outside – boys and girls alike. It wasn't until I started 'feathering' (growing pubic hair) that the adults decided it was time grant some privacy to this routine and they built a washroom out of some salvaged corrugated zinc sheets.

On the evenings that my mother cooked dinner, we would all gather in a jostling mass around the old makeshift kitchen outside, which stood near to where we would bathe. After we had collected our dinner, we would each find a somewhat comfortable stone to sit on and eat. There were always dogs around, so our mealtime was filled with as much dog's breath as food. As soon as we got our meal, we would try to eat as quickly as possible, with the hope that someone else would 'buss' (be full) so that we could help them finish their meal. There was no TV to watch after dinner, so we stayed outside, sitting on the stones and making jokes with one another or taking turns to make up ghost stories. Since we had no electricity, we bottled up the dancing fireflies we called 'Peanie Wallie' to chase the blackness away from around us. Finally, when we were too tired to stay up any longer, we would retreat to the dank and cramped bed. I was always among the last to stay up, simply because I despised the sleeping arrangements.

We had a sparse wardrobe and the few pieces we had were all hand-me-downs. Each of us had one pair of good shoes, and this was the pair we would wear only to church - school was attended bare-footed. There was also only one uniform for each of us, which was the required outfit for primary school attendance, so we had to wash the white blouse every day. We attended the local public school, where our classrooms were always overcrowded. I can remember attending my fourth grade studies alongside more than fifty other pupils crammed into the overly boisterous room. I'm sure the teachers did their best in this situation, but they always moved the lessons along according to the brightest students' progress, meaning the slower students (like me) were often left behind. Even so, I did my best to keep up. We walked to school like every other child in the district; it was only the ones who went to school outside of our area that were driven. For us, lunch usually consisted of fried egg and bread, which had been placed in a brown paper bag along with a mixture of sugar water and lime as our drink. Unfortunately, by the time lunchtime rolled around at mid-day the egg would have begun to smell really unpleasant. Sometimes, I would hide my lunch in the bushes near the school and use an object to mark its spot so that I could find it at lunchtime. I never realised the prevalency at that time of mongoose or rats in the bushes; if I knew then what I know now about all the viciously hungry creatures living around us, I would never have done such a thing!

There were times when there was no food in our house to pack for lunch at school and I was left with two choices, go without or stay home. I always chose the go-without option, trying instead to ward off the eventual hunger by eating as hefty a breakfast as possible – although this strategy was a challenge and sometimes completely infeasible. Occasionally, we could come home for a lunch of overnight-roasted dumpling. These dumplings are traditional simple food in Jamaica, made from a paste of flour, water and salt that has been rolled into a spherical shape and then fried or boiled. The ones we ate had been boiled and then left overnight and cooked on a coal fire; the end result was a roasted dumpling that had absorbed most of the charcoal it had been cooked upon. My mother would serve these roasted dumplings with mint tea. We would rush through the meal, drink some water and run back to school so that we wouldn't miss the afternoon classes.

Truth be told, though, by the time I would reach the school I was already hungry again. This was one of those little life lessons that no matter how much effort I put in, very little of my hunger for a better life would be satisfied while I remained reliant on someone else. At the end of each school, day we would rush home, not because we were excited to play evening games with one another, but because we had a pile of chores waiting for us. We did, however, entertain ourselves along the walk home, usually by playing cricket or catch with sour oranges. Sometimes, we would steal some precious minutes to play this game called 'stuck', in which two of us would stand at opposite ends, facing each other, with a third one of us in the middle and trying to 'site' (dodge) a ball (or whatever object we could find for throwing) that was thrown between the first two. We always played these games in the middle of a road, the passing cars blowing their horns to send us scattering out of their way. Thankfully, none of us were ever hurt!

It was the custom of the children from our school to gather in little groups to walk home together. I yearned to find that perfect group to which I fit in, but I was always on the periphery of anyone that I tried to join. Mostly, I was pushed aside by a teasing remark about how I was always getting good grades at school. That was just the start, though. At times, some of the harsher girls would lay wait for me to inflict some type of physical torment; it was an easy escape if they were only intending to pull my hair or spit on me, but things got more challenging when they decided to wallop me as a gang with their punching fists and kicking feet. The times that they beat me up, I never tattled. I would just hobble home and pretend to my mother that I had a hard fall or something else clumsy; I gave these self-deprecating excuses for my dirty uniform because I didn't want her to get into any more quarrels with anyone in the district. These types of raucous spats between neighbours were common, and boy did I hate them! Since I never was a tattletale, though, the bullying went on for a few years, becoming worse when I reached grade five and became more serious about my schoolwork.

As kids, we would roam the entire district and no place was out of bounds for us. We would go searching for fruits, like mangoes, and climb any tree that promised a good view regardless of how tall it might be. I was a tomboy and held no interest in dolls. I was much more interested in all of the energetic things that the boys were doing, possibly because my closest sibling in age was a boy and we went almost everywhere together. We would often hang out with his friends, who were mainly boys. We would go fishing and hunting for birds - just about anything that was an outdoor adventure; there were no limits, as long as we stayed out of trouble.

My brother and I had daily outdoor adventures, because we had to hunt for food to snack on if we got hungry between meals. When I see children today, who are never far away from a filled refrigerator and go around laden with the latest technological gadgets, I am shocked to consider how humble our lives were. We made most of our own toys from whatever we could find. We used to collect the sour oranges that were unfit to eat to make wheels for play-trucks. We would gather empty drink boxes to serve as the people in the trucks. By attaching strings to the front of the play trucks, we could pull our 'cars filled with people' up and down the road. We also used to make a trap called a 'calaban'. This was a rectangular box made out of wicker that we had woven from whatever pliable wood we could find and used to catch birds. We would prop it upside down on a stick, to hold it up, and scatter seeds leading inside it to bait the birds into it. We would hide nearby and watch the unsuspecting bird follow the trail, pecking away and steadily walking forward until it was under the calaban. Before it realised what was happening, we would pull the stick out and entrap the bird. I'm sorry to say, in most cases this bird would then become our snack. We would eat it on the spot after quickly roasting it on a wood fire.

When I was around eight years-old, my thoughts began to drift towards a curiosity of who my father was. I began to wonder why my surname was different from my siblings', who all shared the surname of my stepdad. To make matters worse, I had my mother's surname. This pointed discrepancy made me feel awkward, more so because I didn't understand the reasoning behind it. In my family there was hardly any verbal communication, and without being told, I knew there were some questions that should be kept to oneself. This all came to the surface one day, though, as I was out with my brother and his group of friends playing our regular bird hunting game. One of the boys suddenly asked me if I knew that my dad was the man named Dave who lived only two minutes walking distance from my house. What was he talking about, I wondered? How could a man living so close to me who acts like such a stranger be my dad? My brother, who was protective of me, was furious with this sort of talk going on, and wound up starting a fight with the other boy. When we went home that evening, I casually mentioned this strange comment to my mum hoping to have her spill the secret as to whether this was true or not. She immediately grew enraged, throwing stones, ashes, pots, pans, and anything else at me that was in sight. I was completely confused by what I had done wrong that had triggered this outburst, but I learned that I had better kill this idea in my mind. Afterward, life continued on as usual and the subject never came up again. When I would be out and about, however, I would see this man who was supposed to be my father. I dared not approach him and he never showed any special interest in me but to say a regular 'hello' or ask me to run to the local shop – no different than how he treated any of the multitudes of children wandering past his house. I always complied with his request without question because we were taught to respect our elders, plus he always gave a little token for our efforts, so I wasn't about to complain.

At age ten and a half, our family situation changed drastically when my stepdad lost his job at the rice factory. My mother had just recently given birth to two more babies, which meant that I was expected to switch to a more adult role as a partial breadwinner for the family. It became my responsibility to find my way to a nearby property that was privately held and pick as many of the mangoes as I could to go out and sell them throughout the day. I was anxious about the prospect because I knew that this property was where airplanes would land in the wee hours of the night to collect the illegal marijuana grown in this region. I would be entering dangerous territory to complete my new task. Until then, I had been relatively fearless, but in those inky black mornings when I had to sneak around in the mango field, fear came at me from every direction. I feared being shot because I was trespassing and I feared being taken captive if I wandered into a marijuana operation and that the police would catch me. But, this task was not an option and I had to do it to help keep our family alive, so it came to be that most mornings while the community slept I joined the other eldest children of neighbouring families who were sneaking around with torches to find mangoes in unventured territory. We collected the mangoes in baskets carried on our heads, which sat atop a 'catah' that we had fashioned from a piece of folded cloth, normally old clothes, to help cushion our heads against the heavy load when the basket became full with mangoes.

I hated my life at this stage. I wished that I was the baby of the family, so I could still be in bed sleeping that early in the morning. We would try and get back from the mango walk before six am, so that the mangoes could be sorted and washed, keeping only the most bruised and unpleasantly soft for ourselves to eat. As soon as that was done, I would be sent to anywhere that the mangoes might sell best that day; the location changed frequently. Most days I couldn't make it to school because the need to sell every mango so that my family could eat outweighed my desire to sit in a classroom.

Even with my contribution, our family's diet dwindled. We would eat rice or chicken back and turn cornmeal, a dish similar to the Nigerian 'ebba' or 'gari' or the Ghanaians 'banku'. The only cereal we knew was plain cornflakes and someone had to have acquired a barrel sent from 'foreign' that we could get a small portion from. More regularly, we had oats; they were not the most flavourful food, but they were filling. My stepdad had cows, so he would milk them every morning for us. Milk was about the only consistent thing in our house; I guess that's where my love for cornmeal porridge came from. Whatever we had for breakfast would have to last my family the whole day, until I came home with money from the mango sales. Yet, too often, I was only able to make enough to buy myself a snack for energy to continue the selling day and pay for my transportation back to our home when the market was far away. Sometimes, when the day's sales were slow, I would have to lower the price per dozen just to get rid of them and make any money; after all, any amount I made was good since we hadn't bought the mangoes in the first place.

As I said, myself and some others from my community would sell mangoes anywhere that I thought there might be a demand; on the train rails, in the park, inn the shopping plaza and at any temporary attractions where people were gathering. If there was a fete, fare or sports day, I tried to be right in the thick of it. There were days when we would be selling mangoes in the same region where my school was located and the kids from my class would recognise me in passing.

They rarely missed a chance to greet me with a mocking shout, saying "Mango gal! You are so poor, you skull (skip) school to sell mangoes". At times, I felt like running away and abandoning my basket of mangoes, but I would force myself to just sit there and endure their chants because I knew the consequence that would meet me at home if I ever did such a thing. Around this time, I would have been in grades four or five, when the students were prepared for S.A.T's and I didn't want to fall behind, since I attended so irregularly. I asked my teachers for the books that were used in the class to study on my own, but was told our family couldn't afford it.

I had heard about a man who would be my uncle if Dave was really my dad. To this date, however, no one, especially not Dave, had acknowledged me as their daughter; although by then the word was out in our entire district about this possibility. Close to Christmas that year, I boldly sent a message to my supposed 'uncle' to ask if he could buy me the books for the S.A.T's, explaining that the exams were to be in summer and I needed to study. I was stunned when he sent the books – it was the first time anyone showed me any love. Imagine, a total stranger was the first to show me love, yet I saw my mum and stepdad every day, and although I knew they loved me, they never showed it. When I look back on this situation, myself a parent now, I am resolved to do everything in my power to ensure that my children know that I love them, not just by saying it (which I do often), but by showing them as well. When I was a child, I lived with the idea that my mum hated me. Every interaction left me feeling unloved and unwanted and I still carry traces of this painful emotion even now as an adult living far away from that small Jamaican village.

After I received the S.A.T. books, I was inspired to hurriedly complete my chores so that I could sit under the trees to study them. Unfortunately, upon my first glimpse of book one, I was only bewildered and I realized that this task was going to be as challenging as my daily task of gathering and selling the stolen mangoes. My eleventh birthday was approaching and I saw no end in sight to my daily routine. Little did I know that very soon my life would again take another turn of fate. Dave had begun living with a pretty woman named Sarah. Not only was she the most beautiful woman I had ever seen by that age of my life, but she was also kind and gentle. One day, she invited me to her house. She was the first adult who had ever sought me out and spoke to me like I mattered. I was thrilled to accept her invitation and before long I was at her house all the time. It was wonderful! She would comb my hair and feed me. We would attend the community's clothes washing day together. On those days, we would hand wash our clothes in the river and then hang them on the bushes to dry in the sunshine. Usually the children would swim and wait on the adults to finish. During one of these excursions, while Sarah and I sat in private, side-by-side washing, she told me that Dave was my dad. I was greatly satisfied to finally hear this validation as the rumour was flying all over the place. Here, in this quiet moment, this beautiful woman was giving me an answer to the very question my own mother was afraid to address.

Over the next few weeks, Sarah and I grew closer. I began to spend less and less time at my own house. Mind you, I still did all the household chores that my mother expected and made certain that I did them well, as I would have gotten a hiding if I didn't. But I loved being in my dad's house, especially because it was an actual house with two bedrooms, a living room, an indoor bathroom and a veranda. To top it off, they also had a car. Their life seemed to me the most luxurious, but my only comparison was the ever more crammed one-room shack I lived in, where I still slept in a urine-soaked bed. Although Sarah had confirmed that Dave was my father, he rarely communicated with me and he kept our interactions on the level of sending me to the shop. I felt hurt by this lack of recognition on his part, but I preferred this small bit of familiarity over none at all. Within a few weeks, Sarah told me that she and my dad were going to be moving to the community where she had come from originally and she wanted me to come with them! I was thrilled beyond words, but equally anxious about what my mother would say. When I approached her with the careful request, my mum surprised me by immediately agreeing. I had thought that since I was now the main breadwinner of the family that my value would be high. But just like that, I was being shooed out of her front door.

I didn't have much to take with me, as I had very few personal belongings. When I arrived at my dad's, my step mum expressed that the items I had weren't worthy enough to be taken anywhere. She set them aside and told me that she would replace them with new ones. I thought to myself that if the way she dressed was any indicator, I was entering the happiest time in my life.

Changes can sometimes be laced with hidden journeys we would rather not have encountered.

CHAPTER 2

"We are scared of the dark, light is comforting as it helps us see shapes and forms. Light helps with recognition and shows what lies ahead of us. We yearn for the comfort of light as it provides silhouettes and form allowing us to recognize and define what's before us. Are we afraid of the dark, or the truth of hiding behind it?"

The drive to Sarah's house was filled with excitement and apprehension. I didn't know what to expect, and at times I felt a panicked feeling of wanting to ask Sarah to turn the car around to take me back home. We had turned off the main road and were travelling along this windy road that seemed to go on forever. In my angst, the journey felt like it was taking an eternity. My mother's home was right near the main road, but now we were going farther and farther away from anything familiar to me and deeper into the hills, a meandering journey that seemed endless. I felt like we were leaving civilisation behind. I remember the panic rising again as I silently questioned myself, "What have I done? Why would anyone chose to live so far away from the lights and main civilisation as this is all I knew?"

The roads continued to go round and round, and up and up. When we turned off one road to another I would look down and see the one we had just come off. I had never been so high up, and it was scary. I think the mix of emotions I was feeling at leaving my mother's home to this unknown house made my anxiety of the height so poignant that I still am afraid of heights to this day. We eventually arrived at Sarah's house where she introduced me to her father, daughter and son; my father was not there since he kept his main home back in the district where I had just left. I was surprised to find such a ready-made family unit and I felt like the odd one out. Sarah took me inside and showed me the room I would be sharing with her daughter, who was much younger than I was. The house wasn't nearly as crowded as the one I had just come from, and there was an inside bathroom and plenty of outside yard space. They had an outside kitchen and attached to it was a 'butchery,' which is like a spare room that farm produce is kept in.

My life settled into a routine quickly, but soon enough I began to realise that I was becoming a sort of house-help. I washed the clothes for everyone and cooked the family's meals. Sarah did register me at the local school and I started grade six. All of these changes, the new school, new home and new family, were quite overwhelming. I had no way of communicating with my mother's family, as there was no phone, and I started to get a bit lonely and missed my old way of life. The walk to my new school was long- about two hours in a child's eyes - made harder by the fact that I was still making the journey to school without any shoes. I also found it challenging to adjust to my new classmates. These kids were brighter, and some of them much wealthier than those that had attended my old school. I decided that my best tact was to keep quiet and not draw any attention to myself, but as the new girl, I was noticed by everyone right away.

Every day after lunch, the teachers would expect us to recite our times-tables. I remember the head teacher clearly and her ever-present cane that she carried as she walked down each row of students seated in their desks. She would randomly stop, point the cane at a student, and bark out the quiz question, "What is 7x7?" This would go on for quite some time, with mixed up variations on the numbers used in the question asked. The students who had not yet memorized their tables completely, myself included, would just mumble some guessed answer or a shamed admission that they didn't know the answer. I used to sit in dread of being called upon even when I knew the answer, because I was still trying to stay invisible among my new classmates. I think the teacher recognised my apprehension because I was thankfully spared questioning for the first weeks, but eventually my turn came. To me, it seemed to happen almost in slow motion; I saw her turn towards me and the world seemed to stop spinning as she pointed her steps towards my desk, raised the cane at me, and asked, "What is 9x6?" I can't remember if I didn't know the answer, or if I was just smothered with fear of having all eyes on me, but I do remember my tongue remaining absolutely still. Out of the corner of my eyes I could see a multitude of hands popping up, and the smirking grins on the faces of the kids who knew the answer. I was so angry with myself as I dutifully stretched out my hand to receive my caning. The pain was far worse than I imagined, it being extremely sharp and nothing like the smacks my mum used to give me with a stone. When the first whack sent a jolt of pain rushing from my knuckles through my hand and up my arm I nearly wet myself! The second one on my arm was even worse. I know for a fact that this was a severe punishment because the scar is still on my arm to this day. When I went home I didn't tell anyone about this cruel experience; I was afraid that their concern over my silliness would be a source of a new problem or worry for them. I needn't have worried though, no one paid any attention to my nursing the unsightly wound nor did they inquire about it when it turned into a scar.

As the pain began to subside, I promised myself that I would never again get caned for not knowing something in school. On my way home, I felt sad to realise that there was no point in telling anyone at my new house about the punishment for my failing because I wasn't sure if they would mete out another beating for my perceived transgression. I reminded myself that some things were best left unsaid and endured instead. I applied myself completely to the task of learning my times tables. In every waking minute, while I ate, washed, cleaned, cooked and bathed, I had the times tables running through my mind. Time progressed and I learnt them perfectly, reciting them in class without a hitch. With that, I began to settle in more comfortably at school, and finally I felt like I was getting on with life.

Every time I could steal away during lunchtime, I would go up to the mango market to look for anyone from my old district and pass along a message of greeting to my mum and siblings. I was also very keen to know how they were doing, if there was another baby on the way. Sometimes I would recognize my mum among the crowd, but she always disappeared before I reached her. Those close encounters always left me wondering how she could come so close to my new school but not come to look for me. However, these meet and greets with old neighbours became fewer and further between, and I heard less and less about my mother and her family. The fact that I had chosen to leave my family to join this new one in search of a better life weighed heavily on me and I constantly carried the longing for my mum's love in my heart.

Towards the end of grade six, Sarah gave birth to a baby boy, my brother, Chad, whom I would cultivate a beautiful life-long relationship with. To me, it seemed like my dad worshipped this new little life. The attention poured on the baby made me a bit jealous, and I yearned for Dave to give me just one-tenth of the gentle attention the baby was getting; after all, he had missed out on the first twelve years of my life and I felt due some level of affection. During this time I was preparing to take my S.A.T. exams. I was also anxious about the possibility of getting to sit for an extra post-S.A.T. preparatory test called the 'Twenty Percent.' This test was given to a select group of students chosen by the head teacher according to the expectation of their success in the S.A.T's. I was crushed to find out that I wasn't chosen, but looking back I should have realized that my chances were slim because I had no parent advocate rallying for me, either at school or in the home.

Although my new home afforded me clean clothing, daily meals, and even lunch money, it did not provide anyone who parented me in a way that involved journeying to my school to discuss my progress and prospects for the future of my education. I was acutely aware that not all of my classmates who were chosen to sit for the extra placement exam were smarter than me, but they had parents who would deliver coffee and yam to the teachers. At that time, it was well known that some teachers could be cajoled to show an extra bit of interest in your child if you 'greased their palms.' I took mental notes on the importance of social standing and once again told myself I was going to overcome this challenge.

Knowing that I had to pass my S.A.T. exam in order to help further my education without the aid of the post-test experience, only served to motivate me to study harder. When the day came to sit the exam, I gave it everything I had, barefoot and all. I left the test feeling confident that my studying would pay off with a passing score. In the weeks leading up to the delivery of the results, I saved up my lunch money every day, refusing to buy anything to eat because I planned to celebrate passing this hurdle. The day the results came out I was eager to get into town and see my score. As I passed the local police station and turned towards the town square, I saw a friend of our family who was a policeman. He shouted out at me, "Girl, I told you I had faith in you!"

That was all I the proof I needed to know that I had received passing marks. I threw myself in the middle of the road and started a 'piece a bawling,' as it's called in Jamaica. Inside me, I felt that something great was beginning to take shape in my life and I revelled in the fact that I could do anything I set my mind to…how naïve I was. I was so ecstatic that I didn't even hear the car horns honking at me. Two policemen came out and escorted me out of the road. As soon as I came to my senses, I turned tail and ran home, delirious with excitement to share the news. When I arrived at Sarah's house I found that they all had already heard and had planned a little celebration with homemade cake and lemonade. They were so proud of me, and it was the first time I had heard such adulations aimed towards me.

On the following Monday, I went back to school with a strut like a peacock. I was so happy to find that my pass also brought me a level of respect from some of my teachers who had previously looked straight through me. I found out that my pass allowed for entrance into the DeCarteret College in Mandeville, which was in the neighbouring parish, over an hour's drive away. My excitement over the passing score was tempered by the very realistic concern about how I would afford to go to this new school.

My life back at Sarah's house was starting to change too. I had not paid much attention to the changes occurring in my twelve-year-old pubescent body, but others certainly had. Sarah's son, who was about my age, started trying to fondle me and make advances towards me, but he was not the only one. Sarah was involved with politics, and as a result she was away frequently, but Dave, my father, was normally home as he was generally unemployed. One day, he did something that made me aware of the fact that I needed to be more mindful of myself when I was alone with men, even ones I knew and should have been able to trust implicitly. It was so unexpected when he started a real conversation with me, and I had no misgivings when he led me back into his room to continue the talk. In fact, my heart soared with happiness over this attention I had so long yearned for. While he was speaking, though, he took my hands and pulled me close to him, only to lift my blouse and put my very small breast in his mouth. No one had ever spoken to me be about intimacy, sex or even puberty, and I wasn't certain what he was doing. But I knew that whatever it was, it didn't feel right. I immediately pulled away and sprinted out of the house, gasping in the fresh air outside in the yard, trying to dispel this sense of suffocation and feeling of vomit rising in my throat.

My mind was also racing; this isn't what I had expected a father-daughter relationship to be. I could hear him yelling behind me, calling me back. I felt so dirty, and his voice turned angry. He bellowed out, "I didn't do anything to you!" When I reached the living room, he came at me and in a quiet but stern voice told me that if I told anyone what had happened they wouldn't understand nor believe me and that I would be sent back to my mother's. I made the promise to not tell anyone. This was a promise I would keep, simply because I was far too afraid of leaving the home I had now become accustomed to, and also because I feared the truth in what he said; no one would believe me. It wasn't until I was nineteen that I dared to release this truth to anyone, sharing it with my first husband Tobore.

As an adult, I still see my dad from time to time when I make the journey across the pond to visit Jamaica, but I have not been able to broach the subject with him. It has been only recently that I gathered the courage to tell my mum during one of her visits to London, and I can tell that this is something she finds hard even conceptualising. But if I were face to face with him, I would like to tell him that that single event altered my entire perspective on humanity and caused me to lose the ability to trust even those who are supposed to love me most, but more importantly, it has affected the relationships I've had with the opposite sex to date. Instead I am civil with him...if someone were to ask me if I love him though, I would not be able to give a simple answer; I care for his well-being in general, but otherwise there is only indifference.

Despite the huge impact that this event had on my entire adult life, it had little impact on my daily life at home. Certainly, I was more careful around men, and had to fight off the desire to run away to my mum's every time I found myself alone in the house with my dad. But my being scared of him, even when others were around, was something I kept hidden from everyone. Our lives went on as usual, as if nothing had happened.

My new school in Mandeville was too far away to walk to, so I had to start taking the bus to attend my classes. My bus fare soon became an irritating issue for Sarah. In addition, the bus I had to take ran very early in the morning, which meant that it was nearly impossible to complete my chores before I left for school and this too became a focus of annoyance for her. The grades from my first term were not very good, and I started to sense that going to high school wasn't going to work out as well as I had hoped. I was very aware of Sarah's annoyance with me and I became very nervous and edgy when I was at home. When the first term ended, I was informed that Sarah and Dave had decided to not send me back for the second term because they couldn't afford it. I received no further explanation on this decision, even though our money situation seemed very stable. I wondered who was paying for my bus fare and now feeling the cost was unreasonable. Was it my mother who Sarah demanded money from weekly or whenever she had it? Or was it my father, who pitched in a little something every now and again?

That summer, I received my first life lesson in puberty. I was home one afternoon, wearing one of my old school uniforms and playing in the yard with the other children. We were climbing up and sliding down the columns on the veranda. As I came down one of the columns, one of the boys told me that I was bleeding. I was frantic but couldn't see a cut on my legs or hands. I quickly turned my lavender skirt around and was met by the shocking sight of a bright red stain! I ran to Sarah and she gently shushed me into silence and ushered me back into the house to give me the lecture on the basics of puberty. One bit of the information she gave me stood out, that I could now get pregnant. She explained that I needed to be careful, but she didn't shed any light on how anyone actually got pregnant.

As the summer progressed, I wondered where I would be attending school when the new school year finally started. My inquiry, however, led to the suggestion that I look around and find a school that was nearer to our home. I was shocked by this answer, as I was only a child, but there it was, revealing a deeper truth about my situation – that I was expected to assume responsibility for myself. I came up with a plan.

I asked for bus fare to travel to my mum's and was given it. When I reached her house, I requested the fare to go to one of the high schools in my parish, to get registered for a transfer. At only twelve-years-old, I had made the first step into adulthood, taking responsibility for obtaining my own education.

I realised that even if I got accepted into the school, I would need to pay school fees and purchase the school's uniform. By the time the acceptance letter arrived I had eight weeks to come up with the fees and uniform. Sarah was not able to help out, citing the initial money problems that precluded my attendance at Mandeville. My father was a potential source of aid and although he had done me wrong, I wanted to stay in his good graces. I went to my aunts, uncles and everyone I knew to ask for money to help fund my second year of high school, but nothing came of it. I even tried to get help from the Member of Parliament who lived in our area, but that too produced nothing. It turned out to be my mum who was finally able to find the money for me.

Just like Mandeville, my new school in Santa Cruz was a long bus ride from our house, but at least the fees were cheaper and it was in my parish. Every day was a challenge, but I was determined to stick with my decision to go back to school. By the end of year nine, I started to notice the cute boys in my class. This was only a flirtatious interest and nothing more serious, especially because my mum had told me that if she got any inkling that I was having sex she would rub scotch bonnet pepper in my private parts! That threat was enough to scare me into staying absolutely chaste.

While at secondary school in Santa Cruz, I struggled to eat. I recall loving when we had practical lessons as I would get food in abundance so early on from year nine. I decided that I would study food and nutrition, mainly because I already knew how to cook, but also because I would get to eat. My home economics teacher and my home management teachers were like my away from home mothers; they made me love going to school and I appreciated their care. I remember loving hanging out in the home economics block as they sold baked products and I would volunteer. I did so for two reasons. Firstly, that was how I could get some food to eat, and secondly, I would steal some of the money to help me pay for my bus fare to be able to travel to and from school. I would hate it, but I felt I had no choice. It was either that, or stay at home. By now, my dad and step mum had fallen out and there was no consideration to assist me, and in addition, my mum was not consistent with her giving. There are aspects of how I was schooled that I wish my kids had, such as teachers acting as parents in absentia. High school was an uphill battle for me; it was a toss-up between staying home, sitting on the roadside gambling, stealing from school, begging MPs to help with my education or simply going to school hungry providing I got a ride. In spite of all this, I made it through. I didn't have more than one uniform for school as I simply couldn't afford it. It was a navy blue tunic with four gores (panels). We ironed with a sad iron which was heated in the wood fire my mum would make. There was no ironing board so ironing was done on the bed, but of course we stupidly used to hold the iron near to our faces to see how hot it was. It was our way of testing the temperature, but shows how irresponsible we were at that age. One evening when attempting to iron, I didn't bother to test, so I just slapped it on my one tunic and bang slap damn, it left its shape in my tunic at the front panel. I was left with a permanent sad iron in my tunic. This of course was darned by a local dress maker and I had to wear it to school, embarrassingly. It wasn't a good sight. As a child in my mum's community I hated when the adult and teenage men would bathe at the community pipe. They would stand there in their briefs when we would be passing. They would be disgusting enough to try to get your attention to look at their manhood and when you refused, they would inform you that you are old enough to go on 'cutting table' (ready to lose your virginity) - it was revolting. I would cross the road and turn my face to the bushes to the disadvantage of 'bucking my toes', and when that failed, I would tell them to 'suck their mums' which is the worse swear words you could tell a Jamaican man. Mums are revered. I think such practice was child sex abuse mentally; it was torture.

One of my first crushes in my high school was a boy, who also lived in my district. This, however, wore off quickly and I began to like his brother. Looking back, I realise that I was trying to see if a boy would be interested in me; I had very low self-esteem and felt ugly and unlovable. I paid close attention in my guidance classes. The teacher explained that our class was at the age when kissing became a point of interest, and I was no exception. I started looking forward to my first kiss and began planning how to get it.

Soon, I had my first boyfriend and I felt wonderful when we were together. The two of us would walk the two mile journey from our homes to the bus stop, sometimes we would walk back together in the evenings as well. However, whenever we got onto the bus, he would stop talking to me and this general disregard would continue at school. I reasoned that I must be really ugly and he was embarrassed to be seen with me in public places, so his love for me would only be acceptable in private. The truth was that I was merely too naive to realise that he had a real girlfriend and I was only his little target for the sex he wasn't getting from this other girl. Thankfully, I never fully gave in to his requests and our affair only consisted of a few kisses.

The next guy I fell for was nothing like this previous boy, in fact, he was a man. I was absolutely smitten by his age and his drop dead gorgeous, mature look. His name was James, and he was about twenty-five at the time. The fact that he was from the capital city, Kingston, which was far away from my rural community in St. Elizabeth, made him all the more alluring to me. I told my stepmother, Sarah, about him and was delighted that this subject seemed to pique her interest in me and my life, but looking back I realise what the source of that interest really was. I was still very young and naïve and didn't wonder why this older woman was suddenly so interested in the stories of a lovesick girl. By the time I realised what was really going it, it was too late and I just wound up feeling like a fool.

Every summer the people in my stepmom's district would hold a summer party, and I loved to go. This particular summer I went with James as my date. When the festivities wound down, we stood close and he whispered a tantalizing promise to me that we would keep in touch. In the weeks after the party, my dad and Sarah began arguing frequently; I would hear her yelling about all the men she could have chosen instead of him, men who had a great deal more money than he did. In the last big argument, she had called him a worthless swine and soon after, he moved away to Kingston to find better work. Things calmed down in our house and Sarah started visiting Kingston on the weekends. I naturally assumed that she was going to visit my father there. She would return and pass along a greeting to me from James. I wondered about this, but told myself that she must have just run into the object of my affection when she was visiting my father. Over time, the greetings became fewer and further between. I wanted to ask if she knew if he had a new girlfriend, but as a child who was 'kotching on eye top'. I had learnt to keep my silly questions to myself and not bother the adults.

Time passed and the so did the crush. Christmas came and there was a celebration on Christmas Eve, called Grand Market. This huge street festival gave us kids the chance to stay out really late - it was such a lovely celebration. I loved it when everyone was in a festive mood and the streets were laced with all the items for Christmas. I absolutely loved it. I felt like a child in a candy shop with a bit of freedom at last. It was my favourite night of the year, when I revelled in my freedom from chores and the watchful eyes of the adults. At the Grand Market evening, I noticed a car in our drive that wasn't my dad's. When I peeked closer I realised that it was James' and I thought he had come to see me. Yes I know stupid girl, but I was fourteen.

Very quickly without any words my step mum ushered him into her bedroom and asked that I get his bags. Although it wasn't said, it was obvious that they were together. I think that was my second heartbreak (after my dad's).

I went outside dutifully to bring the bags of the man I had been so crazy about inside. Sarah told us all too quickly to get ready so that we could go to Grand Market. Soon, she shooed us out of the house with a pocketful of money from 'Daddy James' and didn't even give us a curfew. I was, however, given the task of babysitting my younger brother Chad and her two other kids. I was to be the responsible one in charge of our little group. With nothing else for it, we headed off for the Grand Market and got caught up in the festivities until midnight when I finally gathered the young ones and we started the walk back home. A short way into the walk, a car pulled up beside us and my dad's head popped out of the driver's side window. He was astonished to see us all by ourselves, and quickly asked after my stepmother. The young ones answered in a chorus that she was at home, but my voice was a bit more timid because I knew that there was a show-down in the making.

My father drove us home in silence, and even the young ones started to feel the tension of the situation, although they didn't understand it. When we arrived, every one of us quickly scampered out of the way, while dad stood at the front door trying his key in the door. We could hear him angrily jiggling the key in the lock with no success. He called out to my stepmom, but there was no answer, certainly because she knew that he had seen the strange car in the driveway and deduced what was going on. At this point, dad started trying to kick the door down, and she started shouting at him to leave because she was through with him and that she told him this long ago!

Things escalated into a screaming match between the two. They caused such a ruckus that the entire community came awake and started coming to witness the entire hullabaloo. It was so embarrassing. My dad broke out some of the windows in the house, all the while screaming like a mad man. Finally, his energy left him and he got in his car and sped away. He had not paid any attention to me or Chad, and there was no invitation for us to go with him. Sure enough, the time of Sarah and my father being a couple was over, and I had no familial tie to this house anymore.

I could never have anticipated how this break of a love affair between two people would have such a profound effect on my life. But Sarah immediately saw

Ava Brown

the consequence and told me that I would have to leave as soon as possible. I thought that if I worked harder, she would be convinced of my worth to her family and let me stay on, so, I worked harder. Little did I know, though, that I was about to be expected to work in a way that no girl or woman should ever have to resort to.

Following my father's departure, our money situation got tighter and tighter. James did not stick around. Looking back at our situation now, I see how my position in the family at this time was much more that of a dutiful slave than as a daughter. I was at the end of year nine in school with all of my focus being on the excitement of what year ten was going to bring. I was certainly interested in boys, but I wasn't self-aware enough to appreciate the womanly figure I was developing. Our house didn't have any electricity and Sarah decided it was high time that we got some. She found a man to wire the house, but his cost was beyond anything she could afford in our current situation. But she was crafty, and she knew of other ways to get the things in life that she needed.

Sarah had a male friend who would come over to the house on occasion. He was a tall, tramping man, about forty-years-old. He seemed like an old man to me. Now, this man had money and she needed money to pay for the house to be wired. In her mind it must have seemed like an easy trade off. And so it began; she would allow this man to fondle me in exchange for the money she needed. The man started coming around more frequently and each time I would be exonerated from my chores and sent out on to the veranda to entertain him. Sarah would always pick out my shortest shorts telling me to wear them because they would keep me coolest in the heat. I hated those days when he came to visit. I would try to stall or even hide. When his

41

visits became regular, I started coming home late from school so that I could at least limit the time I would have to endure his company.

Each visit followed the same routine. He would sit on the veranda and Sarah would lock all of the doors leading to the rest of the house. I now think this was her feeble way to protect everyone else from having to deal with the fact that the lamb was being put to the slaughter. Certainly, no one would have wanted to hear me constantly pleading with this man to not touch me in places I wasn't comfortable with. But my pleas fell on deaf ears. This man would fondle me, touch my breasts and grope me. Every time, I felt sick. I was transformed into the salary that was used to pay for the wiring of the house.

I was naïve, yes, but I was not stupid. Although, it was never openly discussed that this man was abusing me, I quickly realized the role my stepmother was playing in all of this and our relationship became strained. One day I just couldn't take it anymore, so I sent a message from school back to Sarah's house to say that I would be staying over at a friend's home. My friend's family understood my situation and did not have any problem with me staying there. I didn't even have a change of clothes with me, but my friend kindly offered me some of her own. The next day, when I returned to the house that had become my prison, I was flogged severely. I took the beating with dignity though, because in truth it felt better than being fondled all evening. At least I wasn't being squeezed and probed by some old man's disgusting hands.

Luckily, my virginity was still intact and I was determined to keep it that way. The situation had become unbearable and I made a plan to escape to my mum's house. Although her home was not as lavish as Sarah's, at least it was safer and devoid of that lecherous old man. By this time, my friends from school knew what was happening at my home, but there wasn't anything they could do to help. Jamaica did not have any proper social services to deal with such situations, so one just had to get on with it. I surreptitiously packed a bag and hid it in the bushes outside. I didn't even feel guilty when I had tucked in all of the nice clothes Sarah had given me to replace the raggedy ones that I had arrived with.

I was sure my plan would work, but I was sadly mistaken. Someone had obviously figured out my intent because when I set off into the night to collect the bag with my things I discovered it was gone. That didn't deter me though and I took off any way towards my mum's place. I made it there without any obstruction. My mum was surprised to see me, but instead of greeting me with tears of joy and relief, she insisted that I go back to where I came from. Her mind was not changed, even after I tried to explain what had happened that had made me so desperate to leave. In her mind, my stepmother's home was still a better place for me.

Through my mum's eyes, I looked healthier and better taken care of than any of the girls in my old district, and she wanted me to stay that way. I wound up leaving her house to travel to another friend's house that was located in Southfield St. Elizabeth, about twenty five miles from my mum's place. I was very relieved when my friend's family welcomed me in and allowed me to stay for a few days. I knew this was not a permanent solution to my situation and I couldn't stay there forever. I was still attending school every day, and came up with the idea of trying to live secretly on the school compound; it's no surprise that this plan didn't work out at all.

Eventually, I wound up at the house of one of my aunt's on my mum's side. She lived in a single-room house, which was about 10x13 square feet and was already filled with five people. I was in grade ten at the time and remember one night when I wet the bed because I was feeling so stressed. I felt embarrassed, but my aunt was extremely understanding about the situation. I stayed there for about two weeks until her husband started behaving inappropriately towards me. Thankfully my aunt listened when I came to her with my concerns about her husband and she decided that her home was not a safe place for me anymore.

Once again, I was let out into the world. I thought things couldn't get any worse, but boy was I wrong.

"Even without recognition, in the coldest part of us, fear has burnt from conception."

CHAPTER 3

"True identity for some, at times is hard to recognize leading to questioning of characters and traits, for some even leads to questions about one's existence".

During those last days at my aunt's house fate challenged me yet again. One day when I was in class, a message came for me that a man had come to the school to see me. I was perplexed and asked what he looked like, trying to place who could possibly be interested in visiting me mid-day. From the description, however, I had no idea who this could be and the girls delivering the message made it sound as if the man was mentally ill. They told me that he was waiting at the front of the school and loudly refusing to leave until I came to him; all this, because he was convinced I was his child! I was torn as what to do, but the situation was turning into a ruckus, and the longer I dawdled in indecision, the more embarrassment I was causing myself and the school.

At the front of the school, I found a short, dishevelled man walking in agitated circles. I was with some friends for support and we had decided to gingerly walk by him to first check out the situation, but as soon as we neared him, he immediately rushed towards me. His story came pouring forth, like he was in urgent need of claiming his stake as my father. He told me his name was Ralf and he was certain that I was his child. He was even able to provide me with quite a convincing history to support this claim. By the time he finished speaking and fell into an expectant silence, my thoughts too were swayed and I began to think that this man could really be my father. In fact, to this day I still carry a suspicion that this man planted the seed from which I grew, but time has consumed my chances of finding out the truth. Even though this man represented a new world of promising possibilities, namely that I have a whole other family that love me and treat me with the respect that I never received at Sarah's house, my disgusting experience with Dave overshadowed everything and I didn't want another father to cope with. I could survive without one! When I went home that evening I relayed the experience to my aunt. As our community was relatively small, she knew exactly who Ralf was. My aunt surprised me by confiding that she long thought he was my real father. This was all too much for me at the time and I simply put the thought aside and never explored the possibility in earnest. I had more pressing issues to worry about at that time. My days of safety in my aunt's home were dwindling and I needed to take my meagre belongings (a few pieces of clothing and my single school uniform) and find a place to live.

As my aunt and I had feared, her husband's inappropriate behaviour continued to escalate in both frequency and aggressiveness. My aunt suggested that I travel the short distance to one of my uncles on my father's side, that is, Dave's side as he had played the role of father to me for much longer than Ralf. I was terrified at the thought of having to put my life in the hands of yet another man. On the day of my departure, she helped me pack my belongings into a small plastic bag and assured me that this man could help me. Despite the awkward nature of the situation in her own house that she was not strong enough to oppose, I could hear the sincerity in her voice and began to let my guard down to trust my aunt's judgment.

My aunt made the walk with me to a nearby garage that my uncle frequently took his work vehicles to for maintenance. It was a Saturday morning and the garage was buzzing with activities, all of which only served to make me pull further into my shell. We waited for about twenty minutes until he arrived. My aunt approached him first, alone. After speaking to him briefly, she beckoned for me to come and meet him. I remember that my heart was filled with such trepidation; I had to force myself to move forward. Due to my previous experiences with the older men in my life, all of whom were supposed to be my protectors, I had developed a general mistrust for the opposite sex. As I moved one foot in front of the other, my mind was racing with the question of what was I getting myself into this time? But what other choice did I have? I had nowhere to go and I had to rely on myself for protection. Hopefully, he would not be an ally and another attacker from which I would have to flee.

My aunt introduced me to Gregory, but using the simple familiar name 'uncle' which I was to call him by. I was only slightly relieved to find that he had a very gentle and polite manner. In front of me, he agreed to assume responsibility of me and I felt a greater sense of relief that I was finally in the presence of two people who might deeply care for my wellbeing. Needless to say, I was quite surprised then when my aunt suddenly turned and left, without even a parting word or offering to come along with me to his house to settle me in. I had thought she would at least want to see the home where he would be taking me, so if anything happened she would know where to find me. It was as if a business transaction had been completed; an inanimate object had been delivered and there was nothing left but to head home.

Not knowing what else to do, I waited quietly until uncle finished his evening work at the garage. Even though we carried out the trip to his home in awkward silence, it was a nerve-wracking experience. I was, only fifteen years-old and on my way to my fourth home. Gregory had actually tried to make small conversation with me as we travelled, but I was too busy making mental notes of where we were going, just in case I needed to retrace my steps. I was slightly comforted by the fact that the distance from his home to my aunt's did not seem to be too great; I could make it on foot if necessary.

We arrived at a tidy two-bedroom house that could pass for a cottage. Although it was smaller than Sarah's house, it was still bigger than my mother's and I was in no position to be picky. When we entered, the house was still and quiet. He showed me to the room next to his and said that it would be mine. The room appeared to be set up for one person and I couldn't sense anyone else living in it – my heart skipped a beat when I realized that I was going to have a room of my own for the first time in my life! However, this excitement was tempered by the nagging curiosity about where this man's family was; where was the wife, or girlfriend, or even boyfriend for that matter? Panic began to rise in me but I held silent as my mind was racing frantically to find a trace anywhere in the house of anyone who might be his partner. There was a faint glimmer of hope when he said that a lady washed for him, but it was dashed when I found out that she only worked there in the daytime. At night, it would just to be the two of us. He told me that his brother and family lived next door and that they had two daughters; I focused all of my attention on this fact to calm myself down. The tour ended and he retired to his room and me to mine. I slept fitfully, but the morning came and my fears had gone unrealised; more importantly, though, my trust in the opposite sex was starting to gradually be restored.

I quickly befriended the two young girls next door and in no time I trusted them. I pretended to be afraid of the dark so that they could come and sleep in the house with me at night. Soon, it became a regular thing for them to sleep over; the three of us sharing a room and me sleeping soundly with their presence as a protection. After being there for a few weeks, I realised that my uncle was prepared to be the father I never had. I became more relaxed about my living situation. Uncle taught me how to drive and trained me in the accounting practice so that I could help out with his business. He was concerned about my education, provided me with food, and gave me my first room by myself. Even though he was now the breadwinner for two, he never showed that he begrudged the financial assistance he gave to me. Because I handled his accounting, I knew that he wasn't hiding anything from me in regards to his money and I flourished having someone trust me so completely.

In many ways, this time in my life was like a dream. The two of us established a daughter-father relationship that I had never thought possible and it was one that everyone admired. I was finally content with life and able to have the childhood I had been denied for so long; eating full meals, going to school and sleeping with ease. As with all things in life, though, this time was only temporary. For all of his responsible actions, though, my uncle was still a bachelor and wanted a partner to share his life with. An introduction to a young woman named Clementine brought that to fruition. Unfortunately, it also ushered in the end of our harmonious times.

Clementine wanted to become more involved in every aspect of his life, as new lovers often do. Soon, she started campaigning to take over the accounting from me. She quickly grew more courageous in her interrogations of me; constantly questioning me about the real reason I was doing his accounts and hoping to discover that I was collecting money from his business for my personal benefit. I was extremely uncomfortable in her presence and started staying at my friend's house in the same district. Even though my uncle wasn't happy with me staying away so much, I needed to escape the intense atmosphere that Clementine was creating at his house.

Eventually, I made the move to my friend's house permanent. I know this broke my uncle's heart, but I felt it was for the best. I felt that I needed to be somewhere more stable and Clementine was securing her position even more firmly in my uncle's home, which did not bode well for me. I found out later that the relationship between my uncle and Clementine broke down irretrievably and that he had moved to the Cayman Island to find better work; this revelation helped to ease my conscience since I knew that his situation would be better. Meanwhile, I finished high school and started to plan for getting into a college. The only person who came to mind was my father, Dave. I had heard from a friend that he was still living in Kingston, having made his residence there since Sarah had kicked him out of the house that fateful Christmas.

I made the journey by bus in search of Dave, with the hope that he would want to take any opportunity to make right the father-daughter relationship that he had treated so carelessly. Once there, I was surprised to find that he lived in a ghetto, residing in a small hovel with his new partner and a whole new set of children. The conditions were dreadful! I felt awkward telling him my reason for coming to see him; I had finished with high school and was seeking his help to start college. I braved it anyhow, after all, what did I have to lose by asking? His advice was to find a man who could look after me and send me to school. In his opinion, having a 'sugar daddy' was my only option. He had no sense of obligation to me; he felt he had done enough for me in my younger years. The night had fallen by the time we finished talking and it was too late for me to return to St. Elizabeth. I ended up sleeping at his house on the filthy floor, atop a dirty mattress and covered by a thin sheet. The pungent smell of faeces and stagnant water wafted in from the street outside through all the cracks in the doors and windows. The smell was so strong that you could taste it and I wondered how the rest of the family could breathe this fetid air every day.

While I slept that night, I dreamt that I went to the Ministry of Education and when I told them my plight, they helped me. I woke the next morning with full recollection of this dream, and a burning excitement about this possibility in my belly. I left the house, un-bathed and still in my clothes from the day before. My old yellow 'rayon challis' trousers and shirt were crushed like a spinach leaf, but I didn't let my dishevelled look deter me from my mission to go to the Ministry of Education. This was Kingston, and I was a sixteen year-old girl with no fear of failure in her head – when I am in Kingston today, I am a scared whimp even though I have the life experiences of my thirty three years beneath me! I quickly boarded a bus and made my way to downtown Kingston with determination in my belly. As I boarded I took one last look back in the direction of the pathetic ghetto where my father was living and thought, 'Well dad, this was your last chance to be in my life and fuck you! You blew it!'

The bus arrived in front of the Ministry at seven thirty a.m., far too early for a governmental office to be open. I posted myself in front of the Minister's office to wait for him to arrive. Every time the security guard would pass me he would give me a strange look; the intensity of my determination must have made me look as if I was crazy, but he never harassed me. The Ministry's staff was beginning to trickle in and they were not happy with my loitering. They tried every trick in the book to get me to leave, but I refused to budge, telling them that I had an urgent matter to discuss with Minister Burchell Whiteman.

It wasn't until about four p.m. when the staff finally realised that I was not going to leave without seeing the Minister. A lady came out and told me that he had made time for me to come in and speak to him. I could see him in about half an hour. I began to consider my dishevelled physical state. Man, my mouth stank! I could smell it each time I breathed out. I hadn't eaten since the day before and there was nothing around that I could use to wash it out or clear it of that bad smell. I bucked up and reminded myself that I had come this far and had no time for embarrassment over something as silly as my outward appearance. Soon enough, Minister Whiteman stepped out into the hallway where I was sitting and kindly invited me to take a seat in his clean and comfy office.

I remember his calm voice putting me at ease as he expressed his admiration of my intense resilience. He said that he was intrigued to hear what I had to say that had given me the patience to wait so long while he finished the urgent duties of his post. I started to tell him my whole life story, leading up to what caused me to travel the long distance to Kingston and even how my dad had received me and what advice he had given me. I ended my plea by expressing my desire to become a lawyer and how it was necessary for me to go to college to make this dream come true, so that I can help others who are in my situation. He listened attentively, and then gently told me the unfortunate news that their office couldn't provide any help for that particular desire of mine, but that he could offer me training to enter the career of teaching.

I was not interested in this field and began to reiterate my initial intended career path in law, but he quickly pointed out to me that I was not in a bargaining position. Instead of getting mad or asking me to leave his office, he briefly outlined the positive aspects of his offer and the reality of my situation. His words were not unkind when he told me that I could either take or leave the offer. Well, I was stubborn, but I was not stupid – I grabbed at it! Since it was also my hope to start my life anew and attend school in a different parish from the one I currently resided in, I asked if he could recommend me for matriculation at a Teacher's College in Montego Bay, St. James. To my utter delight, he agreed! I left his office with his promise that I would be going to college in September. My heart was so full of gratitude towards this kind man; a man who was asking nothing of me in return except a full and productive life. The relief accompanying this momentous occasion in my life flooded out of me in big wet tears. I had seen what perseverance could accomplish and I set it as my life's guiding light.

I went back to St. Elizabeth to give the great news to my uncle and the rest of my family. Since I would be living on campus, I asked different members of my family to help me procure each item I was going to need for my time there. This was just before my uncle left for Cayman, and he was kind enough to contact someone he knew in the local bank, Jamaica National, to secure a job for me. Beneath it all, he was sceptical of the Minister's promise and only wanted me to have something more secure so that I could make a living if everything fell through. I was touched by his continued show of genuine care for me, but I was certain that my dream was going to come true and I declined the job offer when it came through. Certainly, this path could have provided me a salary and some prestige among our largely unemployed community, but I wanted an education and a greater stability for my future.

I readied myself for the long trip to the Teacher's College to put in my formal application. It is testament to how eager I was that I had already collected everything that I would need for attending the college before I had even applied! Upon arrival in Montego Bay, I went directly to the admissions office of the college and again started the waiting game. A secretary finally asked me what my purpose was and was furious when I told her that I had arrived to complete an application for the upcoming semester. She asked loudly, "Who do you think you are? Everyone applied back in April. You are two months too late." Her tone with those last words was final and she was set to walk away from me, but I wasn't about to let this rude and unpleasant woman push me aside and hinder me from reaching my goal. I trailed behind her, apologising profusely and not rising in anger to her insults. She laughed mockingly, saying that even if she allowed me to fill out the form, my application would only wind up in the bin. To this, I only offered her my reasoning that trying was all I could do and I explained that it was really only her conscience that she would be dealing with if she chose to put my application in the bin.

She relented and gave the form to me with a flick of the wrist. I summoned my courage yet again to bravely ask for a loan of a pen, which she also provided with an audible murmur. She told me not to spoil the forms and you can be as sure as hell I did just that. Suddenly, the enormity of what I was undertaking hit me; I became extremely nervous, my mind racing with the realisation that I was my mother's first child to even apply for college. But I remembered my lesson from the

Minister's office about perseverance and I put pen to paper.

When I had finished, I handed the document to the secretary and I could tell she was expecting a bunch of rubbish. Instead, I saw a great change come over her hardened face as she read. My stomach somersaulted as her mouth relaxed from its downturned pursing into an easy and calm form. She stood and ushered me from the waiting room into a more formal room, deeper inside the office, and there she helped me to fill in a new form. It was during that time that I discovered the reason for her attitude change; we were from the same parish, St. Elizabeth. We finished the application session with her telling me that when I received my end of high school exam results CXC, or GCSE equivalent, I was to take them straight to her.

When my results finally arrived in the following weeks, I was delighted to see that I had passed enough subjects to support an application for college, even though my English and math scores were very low. Then, when I delivered the results I was elated to find out that I would be accepted to major in Secondary Education with specialisations in Home Economics and General Science.

The rest of the summer flew by and September came along faster than any other time in my entire life. On the morning of my departure from St. Elizabeth to Montego Bay, I woke up with a stomach full of butterflies because I couldn't believe I was actually about to start college. I was full of anticipation for this next chapter of my life where would be surrounded by peers who loved learning and were focused on bettering themselves and the world around them. Yet, when I arrived, it almost felt like primary school all over again. It was painfully obvious how much I stood out. I felt myself being transformed back into that poverty-stricken, mango-selling girl. Everyone else was wearing the appropriate college uniform, but I was still wearing my old high school uniform from high school as it was the one thing I could not acquire back home before I moved. As I looked around the campus on my first day, I felt so small and insignificant. But a small voice in my head urged me forward, reminding me to never let such negative feelings overcome my ambitions.

I was relieved to see that the secretary from my previous visit to the college was the one now processing the new students. I quickly jumped into the line to get registered, however, I immediately noticed that everyone was carrying a pink slip that I had never seen before. I quietly asked the girl ahead of me, "What are these slips for?", in response, she loudly announced that it was the payment-of-fees slip and then asked how I could not know that with an incredulous ring to her voice. Squinting her eyes at me, she asked "Where is yours?" I mumbled some excuse and she turned her attention away from me. When I reached the top of the line, I spoke to the secretary about this issue, assuming that I would again find understanding and favour in how to rectify this new situation. That day, however, she exercised no tolerance and excused me from the line of students being processed.

As the day wore on, I stood with my belongings and watched everyone receive the assignment for their rooms and class schedules. I had hung around hoping that after all of the other students had been processed that the staff would find time to be sympathetic to my case and help me to get everything resolved. While I waited, I met a girl who, upon realising my plight, offered to keep my luggage for me until I was able to sort out the situation. I accepted and made my way to the office upstairs to ask if I could make a telephone call. This was before mobile phones, oh how times have changed! The office staff was busy with their registration day duties and were not interested in listening to my distracting request.

Whenever a lady became available at one of the service windows, I would ask for the favour of using one of the office phones to make an emergency call. The response I got was a slamming of the glass window in my face. This happened so many times over that afternoon that I lost count. When the evening hour was approaching I had to change tact and go into the village to make the call to Minister Whiteman from the public phone box. The call rang through just as he was about to leave his office for the day. Looking back, I recognize this as just one of the many small miracles that have occurred throughout my life, and I know unmistakably that I should be returning the service back to Christ who has never failed me. Even though I was crying hysterically into the phone, the Minister's secretary recognised me right away and quickly assured me I had no need to worry. She told me that I just needed to calm down and take deep breaths.

Even after I quelled the tears, I could not fully let go of my overwhelming fear that my situation was falling apart before my eyes. I was frantic to get her to understand that I had no place to go back to in my district, telling her that the uncle I had lived with had gone to Cayman and I had no place to live. I reiterated that this college was my only hope and registration was closing in the next few hours. She reassured me that she was going to call the school immediately and get everything sorted out. I finally calmed down and went back to the school's registration office.

The same rude lady who had slammed her window shut on me multiple times faced me when I returned. As I approached, her phone began to ring and she again slammed the window shut. With nothing else for it, I stood in stillness and waited. Eventually, she gently re-opened the window and handed the telephone handset through to me. I was afraid to take the phone from her at first, in case she was planning to slam the window down onto my hand in an effort to make me go away once and for all. But instead she simply handed it over to me. My timid "hello" was answered by the most important voice I had heard to date. It was Minster Whiteman on the line telling me not to worry and reassuring me that everything would be alright.

The lady at the window beckoned for the handset to be returned and without any preamble provided me with a room assignment. To this day I don't know what Minister Whiteman told the registration staff, but whatever it was landed me in college. I felt as if I had been lifted by the wings of angels, even more so when I arrived at the door of my room to find my roommate was that very same girl who had earlier taken my bags for safekeeping. Whether that was a mere coincidence or God in action, you decide. I was finally starting college and it was the most joyous event that had ever occurred in my young life.

"Our entry into the world is most met with laughter and tears of joy; do we cry as we are fearful or hopeful?"

CHAPTER 4

"Far too often we hide behind that which makes us comfortable, looking for a shelter from the truth of our pain and sadness as they are too difficult and devastating to confront."

Campus life provided a degree of freedom I hadn't yet known. It was a new and different environment and I liked it. I felt like I had a place to call home now and a new family consisting of my classmates and teachers. All freshmen went through an initiation called 'grubbing', which occurred during the first two weeks of college and was headed by the seniors. The senior students would come into the dorm rooms and wake freshmen up at five a.m. in the morning. The activities they would startle us into varied with each day, sometimes it was running laps, sometimes it was enduring toothpaste being placed on our eyelids; there were all sorts of crazy things they came up with to torture us, but it was all done in good nature and to foster camaraderie between us and the older students. I wound up making friends with several of the seniors, some of whom even gave me a uniform to wear so that I could immediately start to blend in and understand what it was like to be one of a group.

As the term progressed, I came to realise that the students who had grubbed us at the beginning of the term were the very same ones who were most willing to share their food and their knowledge. They were also the ones who were always available to give advice on how to cope with exam stress and campus life as many of us were not accustomed to the workload our teachers were piling on us, or had lived away from home before. All of the students were expected to return home at the end of term for a break from the burdens of campus life, but I had no real home to go to and the impending event made me extremely anxious.

When the day finally came, my classmates were all packing their things excitedly, chattering about whom they were going to see and the home cooked meals they were going to eat. I stayed quiet and lingered around until I was the last one left. Of course, the house mother noticed, and I had to explain to her that unlike all the other girls I really had nowhere else to go. I was so relieved when she took pity on me and allowed me to stay in my room during the Christmas break but she warned me that this was a one-time thing and I couldn't count on it to become my regular situation during the term breaks. I didn't care about anything so far in the future at that moment and I just thanked her profusely for saving me that day.

Despite the grant I received from the Ministry of Education to pay my tuition, I still had to come up with money for all the miscellaneous things that come along with living on campus and attending classes. Occasionally, my mother would send a small amount of money, but this was so little and infrequent that many times I couldn't even afford sanitary napkins for when my monthly flow started. I saved up some old pieces of cloth, which I would carefully roll around the crotch of my underwear to catch the blood; these didn't work very well and it was an embarrassing chore to wash out at the end of each day so that they could be reused. I was sure everyone knew when I was menstruating, especially because I would only wear my royal blue skirt during those days of bleeding in order to hide the stain better if there happened to be a leak. On the occasions that happened, I could always feel it before I saw it. So, I would wait until the classroom had emptied out and then I would walk by myself to my room, using my books to cover my bottom.

I quickly made friends and involved myself in all sorts of activities which helped to keep me occupied during all hours after all, I didn't have the hours of chores to attend to that I used to have when I was attending secondary or primary school. I found that the social activities also served to keep all of my negative thoughts at bay. My closest friend at that time was Jenn. She quickly proved herself to be someone I could trust and confide in. We were like kindred spirits, as we had come from similar backgrounds. I was shocked, and a bit thrilled, to find out that she too had nowhere to live. It was when I was on campus rushing to get to class that I met the man who was to become my first husband, though I had no clue of it at the time. His name was Tobore and he was an extremely attractive guy, with freckles and just the most handsome, youthful face I had ever seen.

We all hung out as friends on many occasions and although I thought he was terribly handsome, I did not see him as someone I would have a relationship with. As a matter of fact, I didn't think a guy like that would have any interest in someone like me; at this stage of my life, my self-esteem was non-existent. Jenn, however, was convinced that he liked me from the very start. I had even tried to set him up with one of my other classmates - a pretty girl named Syria - just to prove Jenn's insinuations wrong. I was steadfastly refusing to let anything interfere with my college education as it was all I could count on to secure my future.

When the summer arrived that year, Jenn and I were literally chased off campus by our house mother. With neither of us having any need to return to our districts, together we rented a single room in a house owned by a man named Mr. Brown in Catherine Hall, Montego Bay. Over the next few months, he grew to be a surrogate father to the two of us. He knew that we could not afford the rent or food, but he let us stay and fed us anyway, accepting any amount that we could afford to pay him from the odd jobs we found around the city.

That was how we survived the summer of 1994. At times, we would laugh or cry at the irony of our situation. Here we were, training to educate the next generations of our communities so that they could be successful and live full lives, but we were practically homeless. We would stay up late at night and talk about our dreams and goals; how we looked forward to the start of our second year. I knew that my grant from the Ministry of Education was limited to my first year, so I had to start applying for grants and tuition assistance. In a short time, I secured a student loan from the Students' Loan Bureau. Even though this was not free money and the loan was to be paid back after I graduated, securing it eased my fears about not being able to complete my education.

A few weeks into my second year, my mum contacted me to say that the man I had always claimed as my father, Dave, was petitioning the courts to have a change made on my birth certificate. I immediately assumed this somehow had to do with him denying me, but instead she told me that he wanted to give me his last name. What was the attraction I wondered? I had always used my mother's last name as someone who was thought of as a shameful mark of being a truly fatherless child that no man wanted to claim as his own flesh and blood. Now, at seventeen years-old, I considered the idea with a more rational mind. I realised that I had survived this long without having a paternal family name or the favours that I thought that would have brought. While this gesture was not the cause of any great celebration on my part, I could not bring myself to object to it. Looking back, I suppose I let the change happen for sentimental reasons; to respect the child I had once been who would have rejoiced at this moment. My new birth certificate arrived by mail and I felt nothing when I saw my new name boldly printed on the official document - Ava-Gaye Beckford became Ava-Gaye Brown. I filed the paper without another thought, having no idea how this change would haunt me in my adult years.

Academically speaking, I was doing well and my grades were higher than many of my peers. I think my successes in the classroom were largely due to the fact that I stayed on campus over the weekends, with nothing else to do but study, while many of the other girls went on trips or travelled home. One evening, I was completing some coursework in the computer lab when Tobore appeared. I asked why he was not out with our friend Syria who I had arranged a date with for him and was shocked by his bold reply "I'm not interested in her. Don't you know that you are the one I am interested in?"

Tobore's confession awoke something inside of me and I almost instantaneously realised that I had feelings for him too. The fact that we immediately started dating came as no surprise to Jenn. My relationship with Tobore had many unexpected benefits. My whole life seemed to become easier, more pleasurable and I was now seeing the sunshine in the sky instead of the clouds and the flowers covering the ground instead of the weeds. We spent all of our spare time together. He was my escape, my new everything. My friends started teasing me saying that I was no longer available.

At the beginning, I worried that my new found relationship might act as a distraction from my studies, but I managed to remain focused. On Tobore's part, he supported me and helped me with my coursework. He was extremely caring and treated me with the utmost respect. In those times during the month when I would experience chronic pain from uterine cramping during my menstruation, due to a condition I later learned is called dysmenorrhoea, he was my nurse. I was so touched by his careful attention to me, that I could not help but tell him how much I loved him. This was my first experience of love in any way shape or form in my mind. We took our relationship to the next level and I was comfortable and ready, I felt safe, loved and complete.

It did not escape me that the reason I gravitated towards this man and felt so at ease in his presence was because of the healthy affection he showed me, all without expecting anything in return except for my happiness. It was so refreshingly different from the previous concept I had of men. He was in no hurry to be involved with me sexually and I felt such a relief to not have this expectation weighing down our time together. We cultivated a deep and trusting relationship and I felt secure in the knowledge that he genuinely cared for me.

As any new couple, we were curious about one another's history. When he would ask about my family, though, I found it difficult to openly share this information, as it was somewhat a source of embarrassment for me. He was from St. Elizabeth also, and I suppose that fact made me guard my tongue as well. After we had been dating for a few months we took a long weekend trip back to our home parish. During our travels, I plucked up the courage to tell him about my family and my trials growing up among them. I was uncertain of how he would react, but I believed that if he truly loved me he would not see my past as tarnishing my present character. He listened intently and was very understanding. We played the song

'Somewhere Out There' by Linda Ronstadt, and we sang along to it at the top of our lungs. It was such a cathartic release and he fully claimed my heart.

Tobore and I fell into an easy routine after we returned from St. Elizabeth. He would pick me up after classes and I would stay some nights at his place. He cooked for the both of us and we grew closer. I was doing well in school and I was in love with a man who was also in love with me. He would send me roses for no particular reason and there was nothing expected of me in return. I never had to ask him for money; he would somehow know when I needed it and never begrudged helping me. I had finally found comfort and stability in my life and I wanted it to stay this way forever.

My third and final year of college arrived before I knew it. Part of the senior year curriculum included teaching in assigned schools for a term, after which our practical skills would be assessed by an external examiner for certification to obtain employment upon graduation. When the term of teaching internship came to a close, we threw the traditional celebration that was called 'burying the TP'. This event was carried out as a symbolic burying of all the stress from our teaching practice, with the hope that we would all pass the evaluation and successfully move forward into our adult lives.

Tobore had moved to Kingston to find employment in the latter part of my third year. I was dismayed that we weren't able to keep in regular contact, but I was busy enough with my own responsibilities of finishing up. I was able to visit him in Kingston once or twice during this time, but the fact that he was living at his sister's house was an added strain on our relationship because it was inappropriate for us to stay there together. When my graduation day came, Tobore was busy at work in Kingston and could not attend. Even though my mum and sister were there to support me, my heart was broken by his absence.

I felt blessed to have my mum there with me and I told her so. She was proud of me, and I could see it on her face. I took the time to reflect on what I had achieved over these past three years and was even more proud of myself. Graduating from college was the single greatest achievement up until this point in my life. I returned to St. Elizabeth with my diploma in hand and settled myself back in my aunt's house.

My relationship with Tobore had begun to see challenges and began to deteriorate, but I had to focus my energies on finding a job to support myself. After over one hundred and twenty applications and one hundred and twenty turndowns or non replies, I was losing hope. Finally, I applied for a position at the school where my aunt worked and was offered the job (with a little help from my Aunt). Someone finally believe that this nineteen year-old college graduate could be an effective teacher! The job was only for one term, but to me it was better than nothing. My student loan repayments were due and I didn't want to be a burden to my aunt for much longer.

The evening before I was to start my first day of work, a call came in from the head teacher of the school. Thinking she was calling with last minute instructions for me, I was shocked to hear her say that the teacher whose position I was going to take had reconsidered quitting and wanted her job back. The bottom line was that there was no job for me anymore. How could this be? My heart sank further with every word. The lady apologised but said that there wasn't anything else she could do. I hung up the phone and crumbled into the deep cries of despair. I had my loans to repay and wanted desperately to have my own place.

After all, hadn't I achieved my qualification to escape this exact situation?

When the tears finally stopped, I began to plan the re-start of my job search, to begin immediately in the morning. However, God must have heard my cry because before the moon came out I received another call. This one was from the head of Food and Nutrition of Ardenne High School in Kingston. She said that she was looking for someone to fill a teaching position immediately and that she had heard from my education officer that I was a capable young graduate. The job would be mine if I could make it to Kingston by eight a.m. the next morning.

I owned only one interview suit, which was currently in the wash because just hours before I had believed my job hunt was finished. I jumped into action, washed it and placed it behind the fridge to dry. I didn't know how I was going to be able to make the eight a.m. deadline, but that wasn't about to stop me from trying! I woke before crack of dawn and at five-thirty a.m. the next morning, I was on the bus heading into Kingston. I arrived at the school right on time.

Again, the job that was offered was short-term, but I took it anyway. I hadn't had time to find anywhere in to stay in Kingston. I considered finding Tobore and asking to stay with him, but quickly decided against it. Instead, I remembered an uncle who was living in Portmore, a town near enough to Kingston that I could travel to work every day without much hassle. The minute I arrived at his place I was given approval to stay, but knew it would not be an enjoyable time. Looking around the dilapidated room, I heard a voice telling me 'beggars can't be choosers' and I resolved to make the best of my situation. After all, I had a job and I would be making my own money.

I worked at Ardenne for only a few days before the same lady who had hired me told me about a new vacancy at a High School, which was also in Kingston. She explained that the job would be 'a bit more permanent' than the one I was currently in at her school. I told her that I was interested and she called to arrange the interview; she even drove me to the interview. Her kindness made me wonder if she was an angel sent to guide me. I wound up getting the job at the high school and started immediately. I had felt torn and disloyal accepting the job, but she had encouraged me to look at my long-term future. The new job put me in a better position, both financially and experience-wise.

Tobore and I had reconnected since my arrival in the city and he helped me to look for a place that I could afford to live on my own. Soon after we started looking, I rented a room in a house that was close to my new workplace. My move to Kingston seemed to be a double blessing as it also helped Tobore and me to mend our relationship. Even though we had not officially ended things, we definitely had drifted apart. Over time, he began staying over at my place and I remembered why I loved being with him and recognised that I was ready to take our relationship to the next level.

Things moved on well for Tobore and me during this time in our young adult lives. I even made a new friend of the girl who was dating Tobore's older brother. Her name was Constance and she was very kind funny, principled and just a genuine girl. We are still friends to date, almost like sisters. She now lives in Africa where she works as a missionary, but that hasn't phased our bond. Tobore and I took one more trip to St. Elizabeth, and this time I was to meet his parents. For me, it was an uncomfortable introduction. My eyes grew wide when we drove up to their house; it was what I considered to be a mansion! I immediately felt inadequate and out of place. Of course, his parents inquired about my family and background, but I had no idea what to say. In my head I was playing out the honest conversation: "Well, my mum is unemployed, has kids with two different fathers and lives in a one-room shack where we all used to wake up wet with pee because someone was always wetting the single bed that we shared. My stepdad is also unemployed and has been ever since his job was made redundant at the rice factory, which happened about ten years ago. I really don't even know who my real father is, but the man who has claimed me as his daughter tried to molest me when I was twelve."

Just imagining the looks on their faces was enough to make me shiver! Here, I was trying to make a good impression and all I could do was try my best to sidestep their questions about my family. The entire visit was awkward. On our journey back to Kingston, Tobore assured me that they would warm up to me in time, but I was sceptical. To me, it seemed as if his parents and sister did not think I was good enough for him. I was torn and confused, wondering if I should just break it off immediately to spare us both the disaster that was sure to come in the future. In all seriousness, though, I did begin to question the realistic chances of our relationship lasting for the long-term.

When my year at the high school came to an end, I found out that the post would not be renewed and that it was time for me to start looking for another job. Finding another teaching job in Kingston proved to be a difficult task, and soon I was applying for jobs outside of the region. I was finally offered a job to teach Home Economics in Manchester. The thought of a move was not appealing to me and even less so to Tobore who said that he might not be able to follow me because of his steady job in Kingston. But we both realised the reality of our situation, he could not afford to have me at home as a kept girlfriend and it wasn't my ambition either. I also felt the break would have been good.

Accepting this new job bolstered my sense of independence. I would be moving to a new place and starting my life anew. As soon as I got settled, I purchased my first set of furniture on hire. I chose a rather luxurious sofa, dining table and bed, along with a few other pieces. In my heart, I was intending to make my flat comfortable for myself and my man. My hope that Tobore would soon visit me was ever present in my mind. I strived to make my apartment look like the home I had always dreamed of.

In time, I realised that I liked being on my own, but some parts of me desperately missed Tobore's company. I looked forward to every one of his visits. He would always arrive bearing tons of presents, but most importantly he would bring his love to me. Our lovemaking in these times was passionate and every minute I spent tightly up against his naked body was no less than amazing. We were carefree, but committed to each other.

My new job was challenging but exciting; I was learning a lot and enjoying it immensely. When October came around though, I was starting to feel very tired and having a hard time making it through the days. Then, I started feeling frequently nauseous. I entered my food and nutrition practical room and I couldn't figure out what was wrong with me, but my students started to tease me and say that I was pregnant. I laughed with them, thinking of the ridiculousness of the idea – me being a mum, it was unimaginable!

I was still at that age where you think you are invincible; the age when something as adult as pregnancy can't happen to you. Tobore and I had never really discussed having children, and frankly, it was the furthest thing from my mind at this time in my life. I was having fun, we just loved our time and I didn't want anything to change that. However, one day when I fainted in the middle of teaching one of my classes, my friend Gloria took matters into her own hands and insisted that I go on a doctor's visit. She remains Jasmin's Godmother to date.

I relented and made an appointment for that evening after work. In all honesty, I was avoiding the situation because I was scared of what the doctor might say. What if he discovered I had a mysterious illness or a brain tumour? How could I afford all of the medical care and time off work? What would Tobore do if he had to take care of me every day while I wasted away until I died? Such silly thoughts from a silly girl! Would he even stay with me?

When the doctor asked my symptoms, he immediately ordered a pregnancy test which I thought was preposterous. I kindly declined, not wanting to waste my money on something that I didn't need, but when he insisted I complied. The doctor returned with the results in a few minutes. I was all ready to roll my eyes at him, but when he delivered the news that I was pregnant, I felt the earth move beneath me. I was confused and disorientated. The silliest questions spilled from my mouth. "How could this be?" "When did this happen?" It was the doctor's turn to roll his eyes. After a few calming words, he dismissed me to home. Yet, he had not answered my most important question: "Why now?!"

"What makes us ultimately happy is sometimes disguised in shadows of turmoil."

CHAPTER 5

"Hidden happiness awaits if we stop to see beyond the now, only that is most times almost impossible."

The doctor's office was far from my home, besides I was so distraught that I couldn't think straight, so I hailed a taxi. That trip home seemed much longer than it was in reality. I sat in the back of the car, not speaking to the driver and simply overwhelmed with panicked thoughts. Being pregnant and unwed meant that I was going to lose my job, which in turn meant that I would have no way to pay for all the furniture I just bought or the rent on my apartment, which meant that I was going to be homeless! Not only would my grand attempt at independence be an absolute failure, I would also be an utter embarrassment to my family and everyone who had had faith enough in me to help me along the way. I couldn't stop the tears when the thought struck me, "There is no way to break the cycle you were born into, girl."

As soon as I reached my home I phoned Tobore and told him that he needed to come see me. While I waited for his arrival, I paced the floor of my apartment. The doctor estimated that I was about two or three months along already, which meant that I was already pregnant by the time I had moved into this place. My thoughts quickly turned into a petulant conversation with God. I asked why He couldn't have let me know earlier, so I wouldn't have wasted my time on the move, wasted my money on the furniture. I asked why He didn't care enough to have helped save me the hassle, why He had allowed me to finally feel a bit of comfort in the false knowledge that my life was finally coming together. A mocking little voice crept into my head, reminding me of where I was from and that I needed to just accept the sad life laid out for me, of being considered a community's property and serving without question. The voice grew stronger and more challenging, asking "who do you think you are? Just how stupid are you to believe that you can change the history and lineage of so many women that came before you?"

Tobore arrived very quickly, although to me it felt like hours had passed. I blurted out the news, my thoughts having worked me into a frenzy and my beaten spirit just waiting for the next awful thing to happen – him leaving me. To my great surprise, however, he took the news much better than I had. A giant smile spread across his face. He was excited, but I was baffled about what he could possibly find exciting about my predicament. As he said soothing words to calm me down, my mind continued to work. I reflected on the opposite roles that a man and a woman played in this situation of life. Really, a man had nothing to lose when a girlfriend (not a wife) told him she was pregnant with his child. He would still have his job and he wouldn't lose his figure. Oh, I hadn't even thought about that aspect yet – I was about to lose the perfect taut young body and wicked curves that I suddenly realised I had never truly appreciated. I instinctively put my hand on my belly and thought about how men don't have to face the massive changes that come with carrying a baby. I wondered if he would love me after I became all pudgy and round, after giving birth to his child.

As Tobore continued to hold me close and reassure me, I began to calm down. That night, he made such tender love to me that I felt my heart might burst. His arms made me feel secure and I began to believe that things would work out after all. We lay in bed deep into the night, tangled in each other's arms, discussing what would happen next. As the morning hours came upon us, we came to the decision that I would move back to Kingston; there really was no other option, but a part of me resented this because I still desperately wanted to be independent and live on my own. I was also confused and a bit ashamed by the childish desire to simply want to run home to a mum that could give me the nurturing that I needed at that moment, but that wasn't an option either since my mother wasn't a loving, empathetic, or encouraging type of mum.

Tobore was the person I would have to rely on through this situation and I recognised the truth in his words when he said that I would eventually have to move from Christiana back to Kingston. I was resolved to this decision the next morning when I went to my school and delivered the news that I was pregnant to my head of department. She listened quietly and then informed me that I would have to give up the job as my time there hadn't even exceeded a single term of classes yet. She reminded me that I had signed the contract accenting to the school policy, which forbade employment during this exact type of situation. Inwardly, I was screaming out about the gross unfairness of it all, but outwardly I kept my mouth shut because I knew there was nothing to be done.

Tobore and I immediately made plans for my move and before I knew it, I was moved out of my little apartment and back in Kingston. Upon arrival, Tobore brought me to the large house he was still sharing with his sister. His plan was for me to spend at least a few nights there while we got an independent living arrangement established. However, this was short lived as his sister wasn't very happy with the idea and my heart sank when Tobore made no attempt to sway the decision.

I sat in tears, again overwhelmed by my situation; I was jobless, pregnant and now homeless without the protection of the man whose child I was carrying. I was so disappointed with Tobore, even though he continued to try to find a place for me to live without him. Tobore approached a friend who lived with his girlfriend and their child and they agreed to take me in. Lucky for me, they turned out to be lovely people and they welcomed me warmly into their small home and treated me well. But their kindness made me sad and I felt as if I was invading their privacy and adding an unnecessary burden to their lives.

When my friends found out about my situation, many of them couldn't understand why I was living in these strangers home when my man was living in a large house that could have easily accommodated me as well as our imminent child. I was always filled with shame when I would have to explain the circumstance of his sister's disapproval that had brought us to this situation. A few weeks after I began staying with his friends, I was surprised and delighted when Tobore suggested that we find somewhere for the two of us to live together. As soon as we settled into our new place, he sent word back to his family in St. Elizabeth that we were living together and I was pregnant with his child; they received the news tentatively. I understood the reason behind their hesitation. I was certain they were harbouring an unexpressed belief that I had become pregnant on purpose to trap him. Nothing was further from the truth.

I was still worrying that by starting a family so young I would be wasting my bachelor's degree and impeding my chances of getting anywhere in life. But, life moves on. Tobore and I settled into our life together and started preparing for the birth of our child. However, his family did not warm to the situation to well. I felt a deep sense of guilt as I watched his relationship with them become strained and contentious. I remember on New Year's Eve that year, Tobore phoned his parents to send season's greetings, but after the discussion he seemed sad. I knew that something negative had been said about our situation and I felt like running away so that he could be rid of this burden and find peace again with this family. I knew that they were really disappointed with how everything was turning out between us and with the baby on the way. Tobore would often try to hide their disappointment and disapproval from me, but I could always tell what was being said on the other end of the phone just by the look on his face. Even though he had finally started standing up for us as a couple, it pained me to realise why he hadn't in the first place; the emotional beating he was taking for me was almost unbearable.

I was still working on finding ways to improve my standing in the world and another step towards independence was learning to drive a car. Tobore had one, but never started to teach me how to operate it, so I took it upon myself to learn and I began to sneak his car out at night while he slept. Even with my growing belly in the way, I was soon able to expertly manoeuvre the vehicle. Although I was pretty certain that Tobore wouldn't get mad at me if I crashed the car, I was constantly worried that the police would have my back if I got into an accident; luckily, that never happened.

After living in our first rented place for only three months, Tobore and I had to move out of it because the landlord absolutely refused to fix anything and the place rapidly became unliveable. We also started thinking about how we were going to need more space once our little one arrived. We were blessed to find a two-bedroom house in a much cleaner and safer neighbourhood. Our lives continued to move along and we found more comfort in one another with each passing day. Soon, we began to talk about marriage and that turned into a formal engagement, even though we had no idea when a wedding would be feasible.

At that time, Tobore was working as a shipping agent, which meant that he had to travel frequently and I was at home by myself most of the time. To stave off the feelings of isolation and loneliness, I began writing. Putting my life's story down on paper proved to be therapeutic. I finally got the nerve to tell my mum about my pregnancy and engagement, but her responses, as always, was rather unemotional and I wasn't sure how she really felt. Her lack of response made me anxious and I lost my appetite. I can now see that I was in fact in a deep depression during this time. Not having the support of my family nor of my future in-laws or their extended family, some of whom lived a mere ten minutes' walk away from our place, had weighed heavily on me. I wondered if this situation was hinting at how they would treat my child when it finally arrived into this world.

I tried reaching out to the few friends that I had in Kingston, but they were busy with work. I had no one to talk to about my concerns and anxieties about being a new mother and successfully caring for this new life that would be entrusted to me, let alone about how I was to restart my career after the pregnancy was over. Tobore was as supportive as he could be, but it wasn't enough, I needed a female who understood the challenges facing the fairer sex.

During this time, however, Tobore was my whole world, and I couldn't ask for a better partner. He had grown very courageous, standing up to anyone who insulted or challenged me and our unborn child. He made sure that I didn't miss a single doctor's visit, paying for all of them and even attending them with me whenever his work schedule allowed. I became confident in his love for me; all of his efforts made me feel happy and secure. Despite the challenges we faced on a daily basis, tight money, long work hours apart from one another, the displeasure of his family, we still had fun. The days and nights inside our little home were filled with laughter, playfulness and utter joy. Oh, how I loved him!

I would sometimes get to travel with him when he went out of town for work. I loved these trips, as for me they were a vacation. On one such trip to Ocho Rios, I got the chance to meet a famous female songstress who was my favourite Jamaican artiste at the time. I had been wandering around the hallway outside our hotel room moaning about wanting to go with Tobore to the concert she would be performing at that night, when she happened to walk past us! I had no idea she was staying at the same hotel as we were. Tobore was bold enough to strike up a conversation with her and ask her to talk some sense into to me about the fact that I was too far into my pregnancy to go to a concert full of jostling people. She was so kind and offered me an autograph card as consolation for not being in any condition to go see her perform. This placated me enough so that I didn't raise too much more hassle when Tobore left with his work colleagues to see the show.

We decided that it was best to get married before the baby arrived and began planning the ceremony in earnest. When we decided on the date and made the announcement to everyone, time went by with no word from his family to say that they were coming - I don't know if they contacted Tobore separately to deny or accept the request, he was too kind to tell me if they hadn't. I resigned myself to the possibility that he and I might be the only ones there.

We were wed on March 1998 in a simple ceremony, surrounded by about twenty friends and family, including Tobore's parents! I wore a white wedding dress that had been made by one of my friends who worked in a nearby embassy, who I also taught her daughter at high school. We had had to use a ton of fabric to accommodate my ever-expanding belly as my due date was only two months away. The wedding was nice, but like so many other women it was nothing like I had dreamt of as a child. I had always pictured myself surrounded by a grand court of bridesmaids, my groom supported by his court of groomsmen, the maid of honour next to my side, the best man next to his and a ring bearer and flower girls; my wedding was far from the fairy tale. We did get to have the ceremony in a church though, which I had worried about since most churches frowned on marrying a woman so obviously full of child. We even had a small reception at a well-respected heritage site in Kingston that Tobore had been able to secure because of his family name.

I remember being so relieved when I saw Tobore's parents sitting in the church. The dread that had been gripping my heart in the weeks before finally relaxed. His sister didn't attend though, and her failure to come even though her residence was in the same town was a show of her disapproval.

As for my family, only a distant cousin made it to the wedding. I remember looking around at the small crowd that had gathered for the ceremony and my feeling of utter happiness at marrying someone as wonderful as Tobore while feeling our baby kicking in my belly. However, this was tempered by the realisation that so few members of our families were present to share in the celebration with us. I began to grow anxious again about the reality of our situation;

we were setting forth in life on our own, without a strong support system behind us to help when we falter.

We never planned to take a formal honeymoon. In some ways, the wedding itself was mainly carried out to help ease some of the shame our families must have been feeling because of my pregnancy, more so his. I remember someone asking me if I hadn't been pregnant would I have married Tobore. My answer was a solid yes; I was madly in love with him. The pregnancy rushed our timing, but I like to think that we were such a good fit that our relationship would have survived and we would have eventually made it to the altar.

The close and easy relationship that I craved to have with his parents did not come about until after we were married. I had hoped that once I became his wife, and a legal member of his family, they would finally let their guard down and accept me, but that was just a dream.

"They say nothing worth having comes easily,
Yet we could benefit from balls thrown at us that
weren't always curved."

CHAPTER 6

"Sometimes we go through life feeling broken and something magical happens to change that; like the birth of an innocent life."

I was in my third trimester and still very ill on a regular basis. I had to carry a paper bag full of medicine wherever I went to help keep the nausea from turning into violent vomiting. When we were in the car, I would have to ask Tobore to pull over so I could throw up on the side of the road. Certain smells, like Irish Spring soap or the Styrofoam cups from Wendy's and Burger King would trigger a severe nausea. The doctor even prescribed Gravol injections, but they were painful and the trip to the office to get the injection made it almost not worth the relief that they brought.

I was so tired of all the medication and the continued feeling of illness. I tried on several occasions to reach out to my in-laws hoping that I would hear some excitement in their voices about the upcoming birth or comfort about the natural state of my condition, but little advice or support through kind words was offered. My doctor often told me that my illness wasn't entirely physical, but a result of the extreme emotional and psychological torment I was feeling at the time. I tried to force myself to overcome the feeling of rejection and my desperate need to feel accepted. But my efforts were to no avail. I believed that if I was nicer or more solicitous they would grow to love me. But each visit to their house ended with me feeling even more like an uninvited and unwanted guest. In reflection, some of it though not all, was my own insecurities. Tobore worked hard to make me feel included, and eventually he got his parents and sister to ease up on their cold attitude towards me. My illness got milder when the tension from his family eased. I was filled with hope that our relationship would only continue to progress, especially for the sake of our child who would certainly need the love and acceptance of both sides of the family.

A few weeks after our wedding, Tobore's sister announced that she was expecting a baby also. I was thrilled to hear this news because I was sure that our shared condition would help to improve our relationship. After all, she and I were now in the same boat, at least somewhat. One day, when I was home alone, I felt a strange calmness in my belly; the baby wasn't moving. In a panic, I checked myself into one of our discussed private Christian hospitals and the emergency staff went into overdrive. The number of injections I got was shocking! I had no idea what was wrong, but it seemed serious by their treatment of me. When I became stabilised, the consultant at the hospital discharged me to home with the advice that I needed absolute rest and strict instructions for no solid foods; I was only allowed broth. Tobore was in the middle of a big project at work and felt that I was not fit to be on my own, so he drove me to his sister's place where he also lived. He outlined that I needed to just be on broth and no solid food and I was left to rest in my fiancé's room. However, when dinner was prepared, there was no broth insight. I was shocked to find that dinner was fried chicken from a local fast food chain restaurant. The chicken broth and olive branch of peace I was expecting wasn't offered and I retreated to the room and cried silently. Did she disapprove of me so badly that she would risk my life, as well as that of her future niece or nephew? I left and went back to my place as I knew this sort of rejection would only make me feel worse since I was continuing to be so severely ill. Nearly eight months into my pregnancy, we decided to change my doctor. This added a new stress to the end of my pregnancy, but I did start to feel a bit better under the new doctor's care. We were oh so busy planning for the baby's impending arrival. Tobore and I started writing down baby names we both liked. We had a good set of options for either sex; if it was a boy, we thought of Matthew or Michael, and if it was a girl we liked Jasmin, Tempest, Tonya (after a student of mine, who was the daughter of the lady who made my wedding dress), April or Ginell. I particularly loved the names Tonya and Jasmin. Our excitement was contagious and my friends Jenna, Arlete, Janiz and Violet organised a baby shower for me. When I arrived at the room full of friends of mine felt such a strong sense of love. I realised that I had finally cultivated a family of friends who cared for me and loved me as much as a blood family should.

One day, shortly after the shower, I began to feel unwell. I had a suspicion that something was wrong and I soon had convinced myself that I hadn't felt the baby move in three days. Tobore was in working in town and I didn't want to alarm him, so I went to see my doctor on my own and she advised that I get checked into the hospital right away. Tobore and I had already decided that we would have the baby in a private hospital and we had chosen one which was not far from our home and the doctor's office. Upon arrival, I was admitted for observation. The initial examination revealed that my blood pressure was far too high and within minutes the consultant informed me that they needed to perform an emergency caesarean section. At this point, I knew I had to phone Tobore and tell him what was about to happen. When I reached him, he assured me that he was on his way and would arrive at the hospital as soon as possible. I was very scared of having to undergo surgery. The situation was extremely daunting and I wished there was a friend's hand to hold.

The hospital staff changed me into an open dressing gown that provided no privacy. But my embarrassment was soon overshadowed by the discomfort of having to lay spread-eagle and the extreme pain of having a urinary catheter inserted without any aesthetic. I cried and prayed for it all to be over soon. Just as they finished prepping me for surgery, Tobore arrived. He was allowed to walk alongside my gurney, holding my hand, up to the entrance of the surgical theatre. I will never forget the feel of his kiss or the smell of his sweet sweaty brow as he leaned over to kiss me. He whispered that he loved me and assured me that he would see me in a bit. I was sure I was going to die and that this had been my goodbye kiss.

The anaesthesiologist told me she would give me something that would make me feel sleepy and that I would soon fall into a deep sleep. As she started her work on me, I anxiously looked around the room and was horrified to see all the apparatus waiting for unknown uses; I broke out in a cold sweat. I had never been given an anaesthetic before and I kept thinking of the stories of people who were given a general aesthetic and never woke up. I tried desperately to calm myself down by thinking about the moment I was going to see the beautiful face of my child for the first time. Everyone had speculated that I was going to have a son based on their assessment of my belly shape and other body signs that I didn't understand. I conjured up the image of my beautiful baby boy and welcoming him into the world and this was the last thought I had before everything went dark.

I awoke in a haze. My thoughts were so muddled, but there was a definite recognition of pain in my belly. It felt like I had been chopped with a machete right through my lower abdomen wall. I could tell that someone was talking to me but the words being spoken made no sense to me. I could make out a jolly voice saying, "You have a lovely girl!" I told myself I must be dreaming and that I should go back to sleep to await the announcement of a boy. I fell back into the solid darkness of unconsciousness. I was then aware of the jostling of the bed as a porter transported me to a room for post-surgery recovery. I awoke just enough to ask this person to please slow down and be gentle, only to hear a soothing voice tell me that we were going very slowly and smoothly, but I would feel the discomfort because I had a fresh wound.

Discomfort was not the word to describe the feeling I awoke to. Never before had I experienced such immense pain! I gritted my teeth and held back from sobbing as my loving husband leaned over me and began telling me all about the beautiful baby girl we had. He was so excited; his whole outlook on the world seemed to have changed. He gushed unashamedly at what a proud father he was. I was overcome with happiness and my reason for weeping was now because of our shared experience. I was finally happy, he was finally happy, we were finally happy together without the restraints that had been holding us back from one another and our blessed life together.

I told Tobore that I wanted to name our little miracle Jasmin, but when my father-in-law phoned the hospital to check in, he expressed his strong displeasure with the name. He asked to speak directly to me and asked why I wanted to name his granddaughter after the coldest season of the year? I didn't have any satisfactory answer to give him. In the end, Tobore named our daughter and acquiesced to his family's instructions that her middle name be the one that had already been established in his family for several generations. I felt as if I had no say in giving my daughter her name; my choice was irrelevant and I again felt like an outsider in my own life story.

In the hours following the birth, my hospital room was flooded with gifts for the baby and well wishes from visiting friends of both Tobore and myself. When the room finally quieted down, Tobore took the opportunity to go home and freshen up while I took a nap. He was one proud and happy dad, and I was just relieved that our little girl was healthy and breathing. When I woke up, I found that I was afraid to look at her as I feared that all the medicine I had been given while pregnant might have caused some abnormalities. I screwed up my courage and said a pleading prayer to God. I was so grateful when I peeked into the bassinette and saw a perfectly formed baby girl. She was a pink bundle of joy!

My heart melted when I held her; I had never felt such a rush of unconditional love for anything before in my life. The nurse instructed me how to breastfeed her. I was a little scared at first and felt anxious about how it would feel, but I watched in amazement as she latched onto my breast. Unlike me, she had not needed any instructions and knew exactly how to do it. The feeling was strange, but so full of emotion that my life bond to her was strengthened beyond anything I could have imagined. I looked up to the heavens and thought, "God you have made my life so amazing with this one miracle."

About two days after our daughter was born, we were told that the doctors had detected a heart murmur and needed to have an echocardiogram to confirm the health of her heart. I was still all stitched up and sore from the C-section and could hardly move, but when they told me that my little girl might not be well I was determined to stay by her side for any testing she was to undergo. They told me that she needed to go to a different hospital for the tests, the best public hospital attached to the university, which we would need to travel to by car. Even though I had dreaded the pain associated with walking, talking and even coughing in the days prior, when I heard that my child needed me I got up and started doing all of the normal activities. I don't know where the strength and courage came from, but they were there and there was no keeping me down.

Tobore also became infused with a sense of protectiveness, nothing like I had seen before. He hurriedly helped get us ready for the trip to the hospital, making sure we were quickly discharged and safely in his hands for the travel. Thankfully, the test showed that nothing was to be feared and the heart murmur disappeared with time.

We settled into our home with our new little bundle of joy. I basked in the love of our small family and wanted to shut the world and all of its hassles out. Our daughter's smile made all of my insecurities and negative feelings disappear. I began to view my worries over how my in-laws felt about me as silliness. I realised that I didn't need to be accepted by anyone else's family, I had my own family now and my life was complete.

Our little girl developed a bit of jaundice in the first week at home, so I sunned her as it was recommended as the best remedy. I was still learning to walk standing while straight up and cough without wincing in pain, but the duties of motherhood provided the strength to overcome my physical ailments without complaint. I was very disarrayed when I picked up an infection that made breastfeeding difficult; I missed the bonding time with my daughter. Tobore had been able to employ a day-time helper, but he remained extremely attentive and helpful. He even washed the dirty cloth nappies and bathed and changed our little girl without being asked. His enthusiasm for fatherhood was like nothing I had ever seen. Then again, what kind of measuring stick did I have to compare him against?

Tobore's parents and sister visited periodically, and they all seemed excited about the baby. I was so taken aback by their interest, but tried to hide my confusion so I wouldn't come off as offensive. When I had been pregnant, it felt as if they barely paid any attention to me, so all this time together and easy conversation was very new. I remembered how people said that a baby changes everything and for that moment it seemed like that was exactly what was happening in my life.

I called my sweet little girl Jasmin and she was growing into a fine specimen of perfect life. When she was a few months old, I decided it was time to start looking for a job as our money were dwindling. I initially tried for teaching jobs, but they were scarce and nothing came of my efforts. Then, I heard of a job with the daughter of a famous singer from Jamaica who still had strong ties with the local community. I found out as much as I could about the upcoming project, which turned out to be for guidance of disaffected young people, and took it upon myself to write a sample curriculum for what I could carry out as the teacher/student supervisor. I became involved unofficially on the periphery of the project. I would often visit the Museum where some of the initial work was being done. Eventually, I was offered a formal position to work on the project and I immediately found that I loved being back at work, although my duties weren't exactly what I was expecting.

I started to feel anxious and disgruntled about the work I was expected to do. For the most part, my dissatisfaction was stemming from the fact that another person was home taking care of my baby and I was not by her side. I felt guilt that I was somehow abandoning my child and I had to remind myself that I was doing this job to feed and clothe her and help Tobore who had done a stalwart job of looking after both of us so far. Every day, I would have to take a fresh blouse to change into during mid-day because my breasts would constantly leak. No amount of breast pads worked for me! My body knew that my daughter was at home wanting to be fed.

I would express enough milk each morning before I left and leave it in the fridge. I was very concerned about her health and would not allow any type of formula to be used since it was mixed with the local water and I worried about her hygiene. Before I left for work each morning, I would lie in bed and Tobore would fetch Jasmin for me so that I could feed her a good first meal for the day. She would stay on the breast for two hours sometimes, but the routine would get tiresome when she was on a marathon feeding streak. The intimacy of bonding with my child through breastfeeding clashed with the intimacy that my husband and I used to enjoy.

I began to hate my husband being on my breast; something inside told me that for now they belonged to my child. I shunned his requests to be together sexually as I felt it was inappropriate somehow with this innocent new child in our house. I had no idea if this feeling was normal for new mothers because I had no close friends with children to ask such a personal question. I look back at this time and realize that this is the same point when the bounds of our marriage started unravelling. I am certain now that I had some post-partum depression, but I always tried to disguise my feelings of sadness, especially because everyone around me was so happy about the baby.

There was such a tumult of emotions coursing through me at the time. I wanted to recapture the carefree love I shared with my husband, but I was also aware of my time with my child. I would often come home more anxious to see her than to see him. I would have been at work and become overwhelmed with the sense that my baby girl was crying out in hunger and that she needed me. My breast would become painfully engorged and start leaking uncontrollably. I would be dying to go home and relieve my physical pain and my daughter's emotional pain at our separation. In those times, it was such a relief to drive the car up into the driveway, run inside and wash my hands, throw a blanket across my lap and let my daughter feed until her heart was content, just so she could know that her mum loved her and would never abandon her.

"Sometimes our lives have to be turned upside down and rebuilt in an effort to take us to the God given place we are meant to be."

CHAPTER 7

"I have realised that we can directly measure life by our will to endure, persevere and survive."

Jasmin grew so fast in her first year of life and we soon realized that she needed more space than our current house provided. We found a slightly larger home where she could have more freedom to walk around so she could continue to express herself in her boisterous baby language. I was still working with the project associated to a popular Museum, but I was starting to yearn for a different challenge. I saw an ad in our local paper for a sales representative role with a telecom provider. I took the plunge and applied, thinking how it would be exciting to work in a field that was so different from anything I had done before. Something about all the challenges I had faced and overcome during my first year of motherhood had given me a lot of courage and self-confidence.

Still, I was a bit shocked when I got called for the interview. When I arrived, I was interviewed by a man who held a long career in the telephone industry; even though he readily agreed that I was a long-shot for the job, he treated me with respect and conducted the interview as if he was talking to a respected potential employee. He drilled me with questions about how to conduct sales in the field, as well as about general customer service issues. I had never done sales before, but I knew that being friendly and easy to converse with was my strong suit. People used to tell me that I was a chatterbox, and in this interview, I chatted myself into a job! There was only one problem, it required me to have a car at my disposal all day long, and Tobore and I were still sharing the single one.

I admitted my dilemma to the interviewer, but he couldn't see a way of us getting around this requirement. I sat up straight and looked this man square in the eyes, saying that if I had passed the interview and it was only the lack of a car that was holding me back from getting the job offer then he needed only to give me three days to get a car. I recalled sitting in another office, begging the Minister of Education for his belief in me and I was confident that I could find a way in three days' time to overcome this obstacle. I was thrilled when the interviewer agreed to my request.

I phoned Tobore at work with the good news of the job offer and the requirement of a personal car in order for me to accept it; as always, my husband delivered. He immediately went out and found an affordable car that would help me secure my new job. He arrived home that evening with my first car, a blue Geo Metro. I was so overwhelmed with love for my husband. He believed in me and supported my dreams and now, I felt as if my life was back on track; I had a new job and a car.

I had already taken the test and paid the fee for my driver's license. At this time in Jamaica there were a lot of under-the-counter schemes run by the civil servants. There was little oversight and many times you would pay the fee only to be failed and told to return to take the test the next day, no matter how well you had driven, as this was how the instructor made his salary. I had attained my license though and I relished the new feeling of independence that having a car gave me. Shortly afterwards, Tobore was in St. Elizabeth visiting his parents and I was in Kingston with the baby. I decided on a whim to make the drive down during the night so we could be with him when he woke in the morning. Now that I had the option, I wasn't about to settle for staying home alone to care for the baby on my own, plus I wanted to talk to him about the anxiety I felt about starting this new job and how it would affect my being a wife and a mother. More so, I think I wanted to prove to him that I was capable of driving and taking care of myself outside of our house. It never occurred to me how stupid, how very stupid, I was being by heading out into the darkness all alone with my little bit of experience behind the wheel. If I had a lick of sense, I would have never endangered my child and my life for such a petty reason. Needless to say, when I arrived at his parents in the wee hours they were incredibly angry and Tobore gave me a proper telling off. I did not rise to their anger, as I quickly saw why they were so upset with me. I deserved Tobore's tirade, and his words of anger that were solely bore from his love and concern for me and our child.

I started my new job, and although the money coming in was good I again started feeling that same sense of guilt over being away from the home for such long hours. I had thought I was gone from my baby too much with the previous job, but it was nothing compared to now. I was constantly on the road, travelling from customer to customer in order to sell advertising space in the telephone directory. The company itself had a monopoly in Jamaica, so the locals didn't always look upon it favourably, but took the space if they needed it because there was no other alternative.

One of the clients they sent me out to deal with was a large international paint company and when I arrived at their local headquarters, they wanted nothing to do with the company I was representing. They pointed out all of the non-working telephonic items that they had already paid for and all of their issues with trying to get the company to resolve even the simplest of problems.

And here I was trying to sell them an expensive glossy ad! They were having none of it. I decided to take a different approach and transformed my sales pitch into a customer service offering. In the end, I helped them to fix the existing problems and they showed their gratitude by placing one of my biggest sales I ever secured. This experience taught me the skills in customer service that I would use later on in my career to excel.

That year, I made money like I had never seen before. Our little family wanted for nothing. I began to not mind the expectations of the job so much because I was now able to combine with Tobore to provide so well for our daughter. Tobore and I would always pool our earnings by sitting together whenever I got my pay cheque to plan our budget. Even after paying all of our bills, we were able to afford all the gadgets we wanted. We were only twenty three and twenty four years-old and we were doing better than anyone I knew of in my family or age group.

Things were going so well that I suggested a family holiday to somewhere exotic, as I felt guilty that I was away from Jasmin so much and realising that Tobore was starting to think I was away more than our society saw fit for any woman with a husband and child at home. I had also started formulating an idea for a new business, thinking that we could start something in the clothing trade, either in exporting or importing. I chose Panama for our vacation that year and it was a wonderful experience, one that I had never dreamed would be a part of my life when I was a young girl living in the ramshackle homes of my family and friends back in St. Elizabeth.

Things continued to go well at work. I was at the top of my game, and that year I won the company contest for the largest sale, having secured the contract for the

Caribbean and South Florida telephone directory that netted my company over eight million Jamaican dollars in profit. The prize was an all-expense paid holiday to a large theme park in Florida to attend a company-wide conference with winners from all the other international offices. Since it was technically a working holiday, families could not attend. I stayed at the resort itself and was driven everywhere by a private golf cart. I hate to admit it, but I found the time away from the hectic life of daily work and family to be wonderful. Even though I had to attend day-long meetings, I could go back to the quiet of my private room that had been serviced by the cleaning staff and wait for room service to deliver my hot meal.

Like any accomplishment in life, however, my success only served to set the bar higher for the next year. The pressure at work was intense and the upper management expected me to exceed my prize-winning record which put further pressure on my home life, especially my marriage. I came home one day during regular work hours to find my husband busy at the daily chores. To date, the reasons as to why Tobore and I differed on him being a stay-at-home dad are still blurry. I felt terrible; I had never intended him to become the stay-at-home spouse, but he felt I had left him no option.

Our communication had broken down completely; neither of us understood what the other wanted and we were making decisions based on our misunderstandings of each other. There was nothing to do now, he could not go asking for his job back and I had to work harder since I was now the breadwinner. So, we drifted even further apart. He began to feel the same isolation and dissatisfaction with life that I had felt in that first year after our daughter was born and I felt the stress he must have felt to get home to a lonely spouse and growing child. We both recognised that our roles weren't balanced, but we couldn't figure out how to resolve it and we had no one to help point us in the right direction.

Tobore was a wonderful father with Jasmin as well as a husband. He had dinner on the table very often and every time I would see the plates set out, heaped with nourishing and delicious food, my heart would ache because I knew he needed me at home. It was killing me because even though our marriage was so young, it was so frail and brittle. To make matters worse, clients would often present urgent and complicating issues at the end of the workday that required me often miss dinnertime at our house. I tried to make up for it by cutting some of my days short, but this interfered with my work to the point that my performance was suffering and my bosses were starting to take notice.

I felt trapped in a no-win situation. Leaving my job was no option because one of us needed to work. But my extended hours away with clients, coupled with the growing discord between Tobore and me at home, led to jealousy and distrust. Tobore started accusing me of cheating because he couldn't imagine how someone could be busy with clients for so many hours of the day. We were constantly quarrelling and I had a short temper that was set off by the smallest of things.

I had not given up on my marriage though. I made a concerted effort to be encouraging towards Tobore to restart his career. When he admitted that he had been looking for jobs, but his old firm was not hiring and no other industry showed interest in his application, I suggested that he go back to school to bulk up his qualifications. These conversations didn't yield much, and we never finished them with a productive plan that we both agreed on and would work towards. I think we both expected the other to do their part and we didn't see that teamwork required sacrifices on both ends.

I thought our problems might be solved when my company offered me a promotion. This new position had the same duties, but was based in a different location and offered a bit more money. I interpreted this opportunity as meaning less work time and more time with the family. We moved to Mobay and used the compensation I had received the previous year from my large prize-winning contract along with some help from Tobores father to purchase a piece of land. We saw this empty piece of bush land as the tool to restore our marriage; working together to build our dream home would heal our wounds and bind us together again. We rented a two-bedroom flat near the regional hospital and started making the architectural drawings and interviewing the necessary contractors. We were both relieved to realize that the project was indeed strengthening our bond and we started feeling closer than we had in months.

I was doing well at my new job and my successes soon got the attention of another large company in the wireless communication industry. I received an offer from this competitor and it was too good to turn down. Meanwhile, Tobore had secured a job with a supplier of aircraft food and was now working at the nearby airport. Jasmin was now old enough to attend a nursery and we no longer required a full-time caretaker in the house. While Tobore and I struggled to make our daily life an easy and happy existence, Jasmin existed in a carefree world.

When I was offered the position with the new company, I consulted with my husband's family to discuss all aspects of the new job in order to help us to make the decision of my accepting it or not. I had carefully considered it and recognised it as a great opportunity, but was careful to verify that I wasn't blinded to some key issues that would be detrimental to our family's situation. I was thrilled when they agreed with my assessment and I quickly accepted the offer.

At this time, my sister Kem had sent word from St. Elizabeth asking to come to live with us. She was the third child born to my mum after me (mums favourite child as she had a heart condition that made her fragile and more cared for) and I had loving memories of playing with her when she was a toddler. I knew that we could offer her a stable home life and opportunities that were not available to her back in the one room home that they were all still living in. I felt like the salary at my new job afforded us the luxury of taking on this responsibility and because Tobore and I were bonding again, I felt no anxiety about the presence of another person in our house.

The company, however, was relatively new in the industry but very successful and growing at a rapid rate. The output and demand for its services was much greater than anyone expected, which is great for income, but also a substantial burden on its employees time. I began travelling a lot again; there was no formal office space in our region, so I worked out of my home and sometimes out of the car. On paper my job responsibilities were clear-cut. In the initial stages part of the responsibilities was for a colleague and me to negotiate with local landowners so that the company could acquire their land for our operational equipment to be erected upon. Basically, I saw my job as wining and dining people while I sold them the company's concept, maintaining compliance and being the face of the company in that region. I was good at this and soon was internally promoted to the position of Dealer Account Executive.

But the same problem arose as with my job with the other company. My time at home was limited and I carried out my job responsibilities under a cloud of private shame over my family suffering my absence. Tobore and I talked about it from time to time and I was aware that his family wasn't happy with this outcome. I felt like I was being torn in two directions; my heart wanted to be a full-time wife and mother, but my mind craved the challenges that only my career could provide. Perhaps I was a bit over zealous at the time because of my roots being in a community where very few people went to work at a proper job, especially not the women.

My job satisfied something deep within me that was almost pathological and my being so good at what I did only further fed the fire that was consuming me. Yet, this wonderful aspect of my life was causing my family to fall apart. I was fully aware of the whisperers around me, telling me that I was selfishly sacrificing my family for my career, but I did know how to confront them and tell them that I wasn't doing it purposefully, I just didn't know how to balance both. My family wasn't going hungry, we were secure financially, and I used these facts to justify my being away from them far too often.

Before I knew it, the relationship between Tobore and I had again deteriorated into fighting and dislike. He reinitiated the blatant accusations of my cheating and I responded by losing respect for him believing that I had such low character. We both recognised, but tried to ignore the fact that the fracture in our relationship was rapidly reaching an irreparable point. Tobore was convinced that I had a lover tucked away somewhere, and I began to suspect him of the same. We grew so far apart that even though we lived in the same house, we communicated as if we were separated by continents.

Our rented home was a good distance from the land on which our dream house was being constructed. Tobore lost interest in the project and it was I who kept it going. I would travel alone to spend hours at the site and oversee the workmen to catch the common mistakes that would have otherwise cost us so much money. Soon, I took over the whole project in earnest, travelling to the hardware store for items and taking on the entire payments for the construction crew and materials. Even though I didn't want to admit it, I was building a house for a family with no husband or father.

Jasmin would often accompany me on these trips to the construction site and it was our time to bond. I would tell her about all the dreams her dad and I had for this family house; how we would all live there in a bubble of love and happiness. The workers recognised Tobore's absence as an opportunity to slack off. One day, I arrived to find that the workers had erected a column on the veranda that was lean and clearly unstable. I immediately pointed this out, citing that it would not support the weight it needed to and told them that they needed to remove it and start again. They challenged me in an obvious way that related to me being a woman. I was used to these arguments by now, and I had grown clever at making up some story to cover my husband's absence and assuring them that he was still overseeing all of their work.

Finally, our house was completed enough for us to move in. I was still hoping that this residence would magically heal our family, but when we moved in it was even more painfully clear that Tobore and I were over as a couple. I started dreading going home to the arguments and tense silences. If it weren't for my daughter, I would have never returned to that house. The tense silences gradually took over and there was no communication. We were married in name only. I felt utterly abandoned and am sure he did too; even though my husband and I slept under the same roof (but in separate rooms sometimes) our relationship became so broken that soon after, we both found comfort in someone else.

We quarrelled and fought, but had to discuss our indiscretions and figure out how we could move past this in the healthiest way possible for both of us and for our child. Even though I was guilty of the same offence, his admission nearly killed me. We both knew there was nothing to be done but for one of us to move out. His brother arrived on that Sunday afternoon and helped him pack all of his belongings and remove them and him from our lives while I sat in silence on the veranda combing our daughters' hair. Before they left, Tobore came and said goodbye to our daughter. I felt as if my world had crashed down around me, but I couldn't fall apart in front of our child.

That night, after I put Jasmin to bed, I cried until my eyes were swollen. I had no idea how much I would miss Tobore's presence in our house and in our lives. I realised that despite the undercurrent of anger and dissatisfaction, I loved him deeply and relied on him for our family's stability. We had just lost our way as a couple. I realised that Tobore had been a part of my life since I was a teenager and I started to feel shame that I hadn't properly appreciated him; fact is, neither of us appreciated each other at the end. I thought about how I had lost sight of what was important in the past couple of years. We really were still very young to be able to handle all of the events that life had presented us with. I thought of how we might have benefited from more emotional support from our extended families, but the time had passed and there was no going back and no blaming anyone except ourselves. My primary concern now had to be our child, protecting her from the pain that Tobore and I were feeling during this uncoupling.

Even though my sister was still living with us, it was challenging to keep the house together without Tobore around. I had to hire workers to do many of the routine chores that were too cumbersome for me and my sister, such as maintaining the yard. Hiring men for certain jobs served another purpose of bringing a male presence to our house that gave the sense of protection. We gradually adjusted to life without Tobore. He would arrive every weekend to pick Jasmin up for her overnight visits with him and there was never a problem during these hand-offs. He maintained a fabulous relationship with his daughter.

Jasmin was a very clever little girl. She took notice of everything, and would catch the importance of even the most subtle experiences. One day when she and I were out running errands, she pointed out a house and told me that that was the 'girl's' house' where her dad would take her to. I was confused by this designation and asked her what she meant. When I asked "what girl?" she answered with a sense of impatience, "Mummy, that's where Aunty Femi lives." I eyed the place suspiciously, but when I asked who Aunty Femi was, Jasmin simply replied "Daddy's friend." I did some investigating and found out that 'Aunty Femi' was a topless bartender who worked at the local joints and indeed she had lived in that very house that Jasmin had pointed out. So, I began to get some insight into what Tobore's post-marital life consisted of.

Shortly after this encounter, the company I worked for organised a grand function in Montego Bay at which two internationally acclaimed songstresses would be entertaining. The invited clientele were from my territory so I also got an invite, but I knew it would be a working evening. I dressed in one of my finest gowns and waited for Tobore to come and pick up our daughter to watch her for the evening. He arrived with a young woman in the car who he introduced as his friend. Jasmin seemed well acquainted with her, so I didn't worry. Besides, I was so excited about the night's concert that I accepted his explanation.

The isolated life that Jasmin, my sister and I led in our house passed by without much incident, but I continued to miss Tobore and the relationship we once had. I started attending counselling and decided to ask Tobore to come back home for Christmas that year with the intent of initiating our reconciliation. I had the entire plan laid out and at first everything went as I had expected it to. We attended Jasmin's kindergarten Christmas play, where I leaned in close to him to tell him in an intimate whisper that I had something to talk to him about afterwards. He walked me to the car, and stood by my side as I strapped our sleepy daughter into her car seat. I became suddenly shy and my awkward movements showed it.

In my head, I was dying to ask him to come home, to spend Christmas with us, to lie next to me until the dawn, talking and rekindling our love for one another. I knew we could work this out. But, he filled the silence by saying that he wanted to tell me something. My heart leapt; I was flooded with relief thinking that he must have been thinking the same thing that I was about to propose and that we were really going to be a family again. My relief turned to shock though when he said, "I have gotten someone pregnant, the girl you met the other day in fact. I wanted to be the first one to tell you. I didn't want you to hear it first from anyone else."

I don't think I even responded. I was so shocked, I couldn't even speak. I started the drive home and that is when the tears and anger came. I didn't know what to do, but like a child tattling on a friend who had offended me I phoned my mother-in-law and told her that her son had gotten someone else pregnant. Her response made me fume even more, but I had no argument to counter her when she said, "until I hear it from my son I won't believe it."

Suddenly, certain things from our past became clearer to me. Our separation was no surprise to many of our friends and family, and neither would the news of his impending fatherhood be.

When we arrived back at the house, I handed Jasmin over to the care of our helper and my sister. I made my way to the kitchen and began drinking every bit of alcohol I could find. Within hours, I was an incoherent mess, on the edge of eternal unconsciousness. My sister got me to the hospital, where the doctors pumped my stomach to remove what alcohol hadn't yet been absorbed and try to save my life. They kept me in the hospital under observation for a few days. I found out they were going to discharge me on a day that my sister was working and our helper had the day off. A friend of mine brought my car and Jasmin to the hospital to pick me up, but I needed to drop her off at home first. The next day another female friend of mine called me in great distress. She wanted to talk, so I invited her over as not only did I have something to tell her, but I could use some distractions from my own problem. We spent the day cooking, laughing, crying talking about men and burying our sorrows in each other's friendship. It was getting late so I dropped her home to rush back to start preparation for work the next day.

It was around seven pm when Jasmin and I finally pulled into the driveway of our house. I had been talking on the mobile phone with another friend and I told him that I would call back as soon as I got inside and got Jasmin settled down. I had the phone still cradled between my shoulder and my ear and was holding a sleeping Jasmin in one arm while starting to open the front door with the other when I felt something cold and metal press hard against the side of my neck. My eyes swung to the side and saw the muzzle of a gun and four men with their eyes trained on my frightened face. In a second, one of them swiped the phone from my ear while another took Jasmin from my grasp; it was a miracle she didn't wake. The one with the gun pointed at me grabbed my arm harshly and pushed me forward, instructing me in a quiet sadistic voice to open the grill in front of our front door. The two other men who had been silent so far stepped forward and told me to give them the cash card for my bank account. As soon as they had the card, those two left and the other two hustled me into the house. I was escorted by gunpoint to the bedroom and I saw the other man put Jasmin down on the sofa where she just curled up and continued sleeping.

The two men were hurling all sorts of insults at me and started recklessly wandering throughout the rest of the house. They would stop occasionally and pour out little packets of cocaine, which they snorted in front of me unashamedly. I was absolutely certain that I was going to die and my thoughts turned to how I could save the lives of my daughter and my sister, who would be coming home from work any moment. When the men were out of the room and on one of their rampages through the house, I snuck a call through to her and left a message to not come home and to call the police. I hung up just in time before the men returned to ask me for the keys to unlock all of the stores that my company owned. I began to think that this was a robbery based on my job.

I told the men that I didn't have any of the store keys, explaining that I wasn't responsible for that part of the operations. I told them that I only supervised the stores. I went into a babbling explanation of how the company was structured but the taller one cut me off with a sharp laugh. "We're not here for your work!" he yelled. I was shocked into silence, my mouth hanging open mid-sentence. He got very serious and looked me straight in the eye and told me in a hissing voice that he had sent them to kill me. I made a panicked plea for my life, telling him that I would pay him more than the person who sent him if only he would spare my life. He said that he had already accepted the payment to kill me and he was a man of his word and would not renege on his contract.

The man started asking me to tell him about the man he had been told I was seeing. I told him I wasn't seeing anyone, but he said that he didn't believe me. He stalked around the bedroom, saying that I must have pictures of me and this man together, but there weren't any of this imagined relationship to be found. He said that I seemed like a nice girl, nothing like the cold bitch he was told that I was. The other man pushed me back onto the bed and pointed the gun directly at my chest; I knew my life was about to end. Back in the living room, however, my daughter had finally awakened. She was so innocent and curious at two years-old and came running into the room to see what her mummy was doing. The guy with the gun spun around and trained the gun on her; my heart skipped a beat, I thought he was going to shoot her.

I fell off the bed and onto my knees, screaming out for him to hold his fire and not kill my child. The scene was tense, but everyone managed to remain calm in the following seconds. The man allowed Jasmin to come to me. She came into my open arms; tears were streaming down my cheeks. She was such a sweet babe and as I held her tightly to me she told me not to cry. I knew that the situation was growing dimmer as each moment passed. The men were obviously agitated and their whispered conversations with one another were becoming more aggressive. I heard some of the words creep through and I knew what was being planned.

One of the men left the room to go rummaging again and the other turned his attention back to me. I told him that there were condoms in the drawer next to where he stood. I was thinking if I somehow survived this night, I didn't want to come out of it with HIV. A smile crept across his face and he said he didn't need one; he had come prepared. I panicked and blurted out a feeble lie, saying that I had a sexual disease, hoping this would turn him off of me. His jolly mood continued though and he laughed and told me that he knew clean women like me were always careful, he knew I didn't have anything transmissible.

At that time, the other man came back with a bunch of keys that he had found somewhere in the house and told his accomplice that we all needed to go to the shops so I could let them in. There was no hiding the danger of the situation from my daughter now and she had begun screaming and crying in a hysterical manner. I was still holding her and trying to comfort her when one of the men came close and leaned in to stroke her baby face in a blatantly sexual way. He nearly cooed when he asked her to tell him how old she was. I answered for her, telling him sternly that she was only two. He kept his eyes trained on her only and told her in a soft voice that it was too bad; if she was three he would have to fuck her. My body convulsed and I nearly threw up, but my conscience was crying out to me that she had been spared; it was only me who was to be subjected to this violation.

Everything happened rather quickly, or maybe I just thought it did. The mind protects you from the horrors you experience by erasing them from your memory sometimes. What I do remember was one final insult during the course of this violation – a phone ringing and being answered and the two men angrily demanding my security code to get access to my accounts as the other two were waiting at the cash point.

When the ordeal was over, I felt as if they had torn my soul right out of my body. They started to tell me about how mad they were at me for making them wait so many nights before this. They said that they had been waiting for me every night, but I had been in hospital; they mocked me for taking so long to recover before I was discharged. I got a sick feeling in my stomach when I then realised that this really couldn't be merely a robbery gone bad as the Mayor and his family lived next door and had far more money and exploitable power than I did. I was only twenty four-years-old, how much could they really get from me?

The two men were tired of waiting at the house and told me to get dressed before forcing my daughter and me into my car outside at gunpoint. The two who had gone to the bank called and I could overhear them talking casually about how they would get rid of me shortly. They made me take the driver's seat and ordered me to start driving. I felt a glimmer of hope when they instructed me to drive down a road where I knew the police station was. I nearly always got caught by the speed trap set up there, so I was so grateful to have the chance of rescue by putting my foot down a bit harder on the gas pedal. But, there was no such luck tonight; no policeman was sitting and waiting to catch a speeder.

One of the men had sat himself in the front passenger seat and he kept his gun aimed at my knees the whole time, telling me not to do anything stupid. If I had been alone, I might have crashed the car or driven right into the police station, but another of the men sat himself in the back seat with his gun aimed at my baby. I didn't give up though and tried appealing to their conscience. During the earlier part of the night, I had given them sixty five thousand in cash that was kept in a safe place at the house. Now, I was again promising them more money if they wouldn't kill me and let me and my baby go. They merely instructed me to keep driving and we went through mountainous and gully regions of Montego Bay, Jamaica, finally ending up in the city centre of Mobay. They directed me to one of my company's stores, but I had been telling the truth when I had told them that I had no keys to open the shops. They were livid when they realised this. One of them slapped me hard across the face, grunting in frustration. The one who I had begun to think of as their leader was upset too, but he remained calmer than the others and told them there was nothing to be done and that I had told the truth.

We were hustled back into the car and they instructed me to drive them to a well-known place by the seaside. All of their cell phone credit had run out and they started using my mobile to try to make contact with their two accomplices at the bank. They set up a rendezvous point and made me drive to a shadowed area. I sat in stunned silence, listening as the men told me that I was to leave Jamaica. "Go abroad", they said. One of them stifled a little chuckle and told me that when my daughter was grown I should tell her that life is "fucked up". But then they pointed the guns again and told us to get out of the car. I started to remember all of the recent news reports from the Middle East, where women were being executed in open areas to send a message to the public.

I stood trembling in the darkness, holding my child to my breast and praying to God for his mercy. The first shot was so loud it nearly burst my eardrums, but the volley of shots that followed made me realise the men were firing into the air above us. They jumped back into the car of their accomplices who had finally arrived, shouting a final warning that I was to leave Jamaica immediately, and drove off.

A part of me thought that Jasmin and I must be dead and that if I looked down I would see our bloodied bodies lying beneath us and realise we were just ghosts doomed to haunt this beach for eternity. I frantically searched Jasmin's tiny body for gunshot wounds and could hardly breathe when I found none. My entire body, my entire spirit was numb. I couldn't believe we were rid of the men and alive after this dreadful ordeal. By some miracle, the men had left my phone behind and I called the police and the friend I had just dropped at home before this nightmare had started. The police had told me to stay put, but I was afraid that the men were going to come back and finish the job. I put Jasmin back in the car and drove myself to the closest police station I could think of. I was trembling the entire way and could hardly keep straight on the road. I don't even recall arriving at the station, the police later told me that they found me outside in the parking lot collapsed over the steering wheel.

"Watered baptism is said to be the only thing to cleanse original sin, thus sins are stained and embedded in us. However, forgiveness is saved for the contrite making it hard to erase the embedded evil."

CHAPTER 8

"I've learnt to let my instincts and gut guide me in all I do, regardless of how things seem. "

The days that followed our ordeal were miserable and confusing. The police sent a team out to my house to dust for fingerprints among the ransacked rooms and in my car, but they said that they were only able to obtain any usable evidence by which to match a person once they found a suspect that they could use for comparisons. I was shocked to hear that the chances for swift justice were so slim! The officer explained that our assailants must have worn gloves or cleaned up their evidence after themselves. He also explained that since the men didn't steal any physical objects from the home, besides the cash I gave them to ransom our lives, it wasn't really considered a straight-forward robbery case according to the legal definition at the time. I had walked from room to room with him to make an inventory of what had been stolen, but found everything was still present; the fancy electronics, the TV and stereo were there, all of my jewellery, and even the mass of cash I had hidden secretly was still in the house.

The realisation that they truly had no interest in our belongings shook me to my very core. I was trembling like a leaf and could hardly breathe when I remembered the man sneering to me that they were simply sent there by an enemy to kill me. Earlier, the police had sent me to a hospital in Montego Bay for treatment of my physical wounds from the night. There too, the doctors had given the grim news that there was little to no physical evidence from my attackers they could retrieve from my damaged body. Even though the house was released from its status as an active crime scene, I could not return to living in it. I got assistance from an organisation I was close to that put the three of us, my sister, my daughter and me up in a hotel and they worked with the police to trace the calls made by the assailants from my cell phone that night. This was a time when tracing technology was still new in Jamaica, so the only information they managed to get was that one of the calls had been made to a well-known ghetto area August Town, St. Andrew.

We stayed at the hotel for a few days at the hotel; just long enough to finish dealing with the police to make the report. As soon as that was completed, I felt compelled to flee so that I could gather my wits. The only place I could think of that would provide a calming and safe environment was Florida, probably because of my recent experience there with my previous company. Jasmin and I flew out a few days after we secured visas. I wasn't sure where my sister went that night, but we re-joined the next day. However, the distance did not calm my nerves the way I had expected. I was an emotional wreck. I couldn't eat and my nights were spent either sleeplessly pacing the room, or jolting up from a nightmare when I would relive the trauma in my dreams. A friend called and told me that Tobore had moved from Montego Bay back to his parents place in St. Elizabeth, having quit his job without giving a reason for his sudden departure. I wondered if he left out of fear for himself after hearing what had happened to me or if he somehow fear of being questioned as to why we were estranged and he now had someone pregnant. With this in mind, my attacker's voice, saying they had been sent by someone I knew to kill me, kept playing over and over again in my head.

The time away was doing no good and I knew Jasmin and I couldn't hide out here forever. I needed to figure out how I was going to move on with my life. Could I simply force my mind to shut out the trauma and return to my home and my daily work schedule? Their departing warning to me was to leave Jamaica, dare I go against it? Would they come back to finish the job? Regardless of what my ultimate decisions would be, I couldn't make them and carry them out from my cousin's home in Florida. I steeled my nerves and packed up Jasmin and headed back home to face this situation head-on.

I was surprised that the love for my family home that I had built with husband was now dead. I stood at the front door and realized this home was really just an object made of brick and wood, nothing more. My life within its walls had been ended by those four men and I know walked its hallways like a ghost. I employed a security guard, but still could not find solace. My sister moved back in and the three of us stayed in a single bedroom. However, I was still too terrified to sleep the whole night through. One night when I couldn't calm down, I called on the friend whom I had spent the day with prior to the start of the night-long attack and who I was on the phone to when the attackers arrived. While talking to her with my sister and Jasmin beside me in the bed fast asleep, my heart nearly seized when my ears picked up an unusual sound, almost like footsteps up above on the roof of the house. At first, I thought I must be hallucinating because of my hypersensitive state.

I ensured the two girls beside me were sound asleep as I didn't want to alarm them. I was sweating and really beginning to panic. As I gently opened the curtain to see if I could get a sneak of what was happening, I was met by the barrel of a gun. I gently shook my sister awake, quickly stifling her gasp of surprise by cupping my hand over her mouth. I whispered that someone was outside and I was certain it was the men coming back to kill me. I feared there was no escape for me this time and my imagination went into overdrive, embodying these coke-fuelled fiends with spy-level skills with which they would swiftly disable the guard and my sister and make their way inside to shoot me in front of my baby girl. I gently got off the bed and tried to get everyone on the floor without any sound hand still over my sisters' mouth as knowing her she would just collapse.

I grabbed for my cell phone and frantically dialled a friend of mine in the police force who had been at my house earlier that evening. I gave him the pre-arranged signal we had come up with to alert him of immediate danger to my life. He understood immediately and rang off. I used my shaking fingers to dial the local police station, which was only a seven minutes' walk from my house. Within moments, I heard the scream of a siren and my police friend called to say that he was the one pulling up outside and instructing us to stay put in the house while he started prowling the perimeter of the building along with the security guard he found unharmed, too afraid to move frozen on the sofa in the front room. Several minutes later, I heard the noises of several cars, alerting us that the local police were finally arriving.

The sirens had chased the men off and we were safe for another few hours, but I knew they were not going to let up. I knew that this was the last night I would spend in my home. The next day, I went to Santa Cruz to stay with a friend and started looking for somewhere to live. Not long after, I found a house to rent in Santa Cruz with enough bedrooms for myself, Jasmin and my sister. However, as we finished packing up the old house and started loading the car with our personal belongings, Kem told me that she was not going to join us. I didn't blame her for wanting to distance herself from the potential danger that continued to hang over my head, but I was disheartened that I was to take on this new phase of my life completely alone, without help for Jasmin, and I was frustrated at her timing since I had already committed to the massive rent for the larger place that she was to have contributed to while living there with us.

I completed the move in a daze. Everything was happening so quickly and I still hadn't had time to really process the trauma of the events or what they really meant to my life and my sanity. When we arrived in Santa Cruz, I contacted the lady who had been employed as my helper right before the attack. I was so stressed that I hadn't had time to consider the frightening implications of the suspicious circumstances under which she had requested the day off on the evening when the men showed up to begin their reign of terror.

My new life in Santa Cruz was the same as it had been in Florida. Every night when the sun set, I would be besieged by the normal noises of the boisterous city around me, picking out individual sounds and convincing myself they were whispers of the men coming to kill me. The entire trauma of that night in Montego Bay replayed constantly in my mind. I was becoming a shell of the woman I used to be. I knew I couldn't continue in this way or be an effective mother to Jasmin, so when my aunt invited me to come to London I jumped at the idea, especially as I was set to complete an exam for the Bachelor degree I was already struggling to complete.

London was far away, but I had an aunt who had left Jamaica many years ago to emigrate there. She and I weren't close at all. In fact, my only interactions with her occurred when I was a young child. But when I wrote to tell her about my upcoming trip, her response was positive and warm. I couldn't afford to take Jasmin out of school, but also needed that time and space from everything to think and unfreeze my zombie state. My in-laws volunteered to keep her and she was excited about the prospect of staying there because her daddy was living in their house as well. I felt certain that despite what threats were being aimed towards my life, no one would be seeking to harm this innocent child, so I entrusted my daughter to them.

I travelled to London and passed all of my exams. My aunt was such a blessing in the down-times; she took me all over, attending weddings of very distant relatives. Before then, I didn't even know I had and fellow Jamaicans who had relocated to the UK. The whirlwind social schedule helped me to start to forget about the stresses that awaited me back home. I began to see that as long as I had my daughter with me, I could build a fulfilling life in this new country. Even though the people and the weather in this country were vastly different from my home country, I felt a sense of safety. The news reports on the TV reported crimes that were nowhere near as heinous as those that had become routine in some parts of Jamaica at that time. Certainly, I didn't hear of anything as blatantly violent as the attack I had just experienced in my own home.

I began dreading going back to the life that Jasmin and I had been living back in Santa Cruz. Even on the nights that my mind calmed enough to allow sleep, we would be awoken by the intermittent flashes of lights being shone in our windows by the police who were still making routine patrols of our house to assure our continued safety. My auntie recognised my internal torment and casually suggested that I register with some local employment agencies just to see what opportunities May come my way.

I thought very carefully about the reality of our situation in Jamaica now. I thought of how I could no longer stand to drive the car with anyone else sitting in back seat, as I would flash to the fear of that person suddenly pulling a gun on me or Jasmin. I thought of how I would drive very far away, meandering to get to any destination, all to avoid any crowded areas where I may find my attackers who would force their way into my car. I thought of how I could never make myself drive anywhere as the hour of sunset neared since the dark was much too frightening a reminder of our plight. This was no way to live and I knew it. I acquiesced to my auntie's wisdom and registered with several agencies before making the trip back home. During this time and on his visits to see Jasmin, Tobore and I were slowly getting close again and somewhat had a weird relationship; he had a woman and I was now his other woman, me his wife.

I left London with a bittersweet feeling. This city was so completely different from anywhere I had ever experienced before, yet I felt safer there than in the country I had spent my entire life. When I returned home to Santa Cruz, I did my best to settle into life again. My company rearranged my responsibilities as my territory alignment was to include the parish I now lived in and the adjoining ones. This meant that I was now responsible for the parishes of St. Elizabeth, Hanover, Westmoreland, Manchester, Trelawney and St. James. It was June of 2002, and I was doing my best to return to my normal life of hard work and taking care of my growing daughter. One day, as I was travelling from an appointment in Manchester back to our rented home in Santa Cruz, my cell phone began to ring incessantly. I had purposefully ignored the first barrage of ringing because the hill I was driving up was particularly steep and treacherous; the site of many frequent accidents. Yet, when the phone started ringing a third time I pulled to the side of the road, panicking with the thought that there may be an emergency at my daughter's school or the house.

When I answered, I found that the person on the other end of the line was indeed calling with life-changing news, but not in the way I had imagined at all. The caller was in fact a secondary school principal from the Mitcham borough in London. She stated that she had received my CV from one of the job agencies and she was anxious to speak with me about current and upcoming employment opportunities with her school. I was slightly taken aback by her interest in me; after all, I had not taught in four years. This must be divine intervention, I thought. God's favour must finally be turning towards me again! I refocused my attention of the words being spoken into my ear from so far away. She was already starting to conduct the interview with me right there on the side of the Spur Tree Hill.

I hadn't really expected anything to come of my registering with the job agencies, let alone to get an interview for a position in a field I had left so long ago. It was all happening so suddenly. My mind started to buzz with excuses to get out of the interview. What if at the end of this interview she was to offer me the position and expect me to commit to moving there? A pessimistic voice in my head reminded me that teaching was not something I had a flair for like I did with sales, or was something that I would even enjoy at this stage in my life as it couldn't afford me the lifestyle that I had grown accustomed to, and mentally I wasn't in a good place to absorb the stress of children in my head. This little voice told me that even considering a move into the teaching field would be a step back. After all, teaching was something I had used to get a start in life and it was not my dream job.

In the background, I could hear the woman's continued questions. Somehow I was managing to answer them coherently and from the tone of her voice, she appeared to be pleased with my responses. Then, it seemed to me the conversation was ended abruptly, with her making a firm job offer and asking when I could start. I was dumbfounded and searched for how to answer this last important question that she asked of me.

There was so much to consider! I mumbled some platitudes to give myself time to think. A part of me thought I must be crazy to not just hang up on this absurd offer and go about my daily business. That part of me was seized by the fear of the thought of leaving my country. After all, the job I held now gave me financial stability and the ability to afford much more than Jasmin and I could ever need. I had just imported a fancy new car from Japan, which was my weekend car. Very few people at my age could afford such a luxury, so who was I to throw it all away? I still owned the house in Montego Bay and it was now rented so it was not a financial burden and I could count it as a solid investment for my future. I was now living closer to my mother and she was providing a new type of emotional support I had not known before. Finally, I was still legally married, even though I only saw my husband occasionally and he had started another family with another woman. My feelings for him were certainly tangled and complex.

Yet, another part of me began to intrude in this torrent of thoughts, and it was the voice of logic. Despite all of the successful contracts, I was still managing to secure in my fragile post-trauma state. I lived every moment of my life in fear and paranoia.

Jasmin and I still lived under constant police surveillance and our activities were restricted. This was really no sort of life, no matter how many amenities and gadgets I could afford to buy.

With this final realisation, I made an impulsive decision to accept the job. The voice on the other end of the line was filled with happy relief as she rolled out the details of my employment and told me the agency would finalise the details. My first day was to be on September 20th. I hung up the phone and stood in awed silence for a moment. It appeared to me that God had just opened the door leading to the next chapter of my life. I called my mum and told her the news. She was shocked, but mostly unsure if I should move to another country, or to stay near to her where she could essentially watch over me. I also called Tobore to tell him I had accepted a job in London. He expressed elation at my decision and told me that this was the best way for me to move forward. The sincerity in his voice reminded me of what it was like in those years during college when he was my staunchest supporter.

Alone, I sat silently in my car on the side of that steep hill for some time, trying to gather my emotions. Parts of me felt afraid of the unknown. I wondered what life would be like once I moved to the UK. Granted, London had looked inviting while I was on my short visit, but what could I really tell about a place after just a two-week visit? In reality though, it didn't matter what my fears were, I had accepted the job and now needed to get Jasmin and I ready for the big move.

Within days, the job agency had already forwarded the various documents that I would need to send to the British Embassy in order to collect my work visa. They also informed me of the vaccinations that I would require in order to teach in the UK. Before I knew it, I had an appointment with a nearby doctor in Santa Cruz and I left his office completely up to date on my immunisations. Everything was happening so fast I couldn't keep up.

My new job did not supply an allowance for moving all of my household belongings, so I made quick sales of the largest items I owned. My sewing machine, a treadmill, our beds and the large American-style appliances were quickly snapped up or given on credit. A few weeks later, Tobore accompanied Jasmin and me to the visa interview session which was conducted in Kingston. That day, it was raining in sheets and I phoned the Embassy ahead of our travel to ask if it was necessary to make the trip due to the rain. The woman who answered my call laughed good-naturedly at my question and told me that if I intended to live in the UK I needed to understand that rain stops nothing. We hastily jumped into my car and made the trip to collect our visas.

When everything was in place for our emigration, I resigned from my job with the company that had been so much a part of my life over the past few years. My heart was heavy and I began doubting my decision as I delivered the news to my supervisors. I constantly reminded myself of the promise of the new life awaiting me in London, one that would bring me out of the fear I lived in, in Jamaica. The plan was for me to move to London first, where I would set up a home for my daughter and sister to join me later in October as my sister had decided she would join us on this grand new adventure. Moreover, Tobore had told me that he would like to come with us as well; his plan was to join us there in December of that year – things had not played out well with the new woman. In the meantime, Jasmin would stay with her paternal grandparents.

Although I knew Tobore's parents would look after my daughter well, it was difficult for me to leave her behind. I kept my focus on the knowledge that this was the best decision for us as a family and eventually we would all be together again. I was more excited to finally have the opportunity for Tobore and me to work on our marriage again, away from all the stresses of our families and the demands that we were surrounded by at the time including his new-born; a fresh new environment may do us some good, I thought. In August, only a few weeks before my scheduled departure, Tobore's girlfriend gave birth to their daughter. The news of her birth ripped my soul in two. It felt as if someone had defiled the one sacred event that he and I shared. It was a difficult period for everyone involved, because Tobore and I had begun seeing each other on a regular basis. The tension was thick between everyone; Tobore and I and Tobore and the mother of his new child. I can only imagine the torment he felt, or how it compared to my own, because we never spoke directly of it.

Here we were, Tobore and I, with a child who, in essence, was the core of our relationship and she needed her father. But, at the same time, he had just brought this new child into the world, and this child needed a father just as much as mine did. I was torn with the shame that I would be taking the father away from this child, like someone had taken mine away from me at one point. I was beginning to feel like I should start a blog about my life and the domain name would be Confused.com, with a capital 'C'.

I stayed with Tobore in Montego Bay the night before my flight to London. I awoke in his arms feeling extremely nervous. I pulled myself from the bed and forced myself into the shower and started getting ready to leave. All of a sudden, there was a great commotion at the door of his flat. His girlfriend had arrived on the doorstep and was demanding entrance. The scene was heart wrenching and I felt an unexpected wave of guilt and shame, even though I was with my husband. She was crying and shouting at the two of us, clutching at her heart and screaming out in pain as if it was breaking. I felt fear grip my heart that the cost of my husband and I restarting our married life would be the destruction of this other woman and the future of her new-born baby.

Finally, things calmed down when she realised that her pleas to Tobore were falling on deaf ears. He had not even let her in the door. I stood in the silence that followed and collapsed in his arms, sobbing. I felt that our marriage had been broken in so many ways, not just by this situation, but by everything the two us had been through in the past year, both together and separate. Our ride to the airport left me feeling that we were facing so many uncertainties as a couple and wondering how we could possibly survive. I could not bring myself to voice all of the questions that were swirling in my head. Could I bear the guilt of separating this man from his new-born child? Was I making a mistake by reconciling with him? Would moving our family to an unknown country be our downfall?

As I boarded the plane, I looked back at the landscape I was leaving. I bid farewell to the country that I had known my entire life. The nine-hour flight seemed to last for an eternity. I watched movies, walked around the plane, and even slept. It was frustrating to wake up and still be thousands of miles up in the sky, with hours left until I was to reach my destination. I fought the urge to stand up screaming for the pilots to turn around and take me home! I was reminded of the feeling I had as a child, living at the will of everyone else in control, but I reminded myself that I had made the choice to get on this plane and to take the chance of restarting our lives away from everyone we knew and loved.

The airline served lovely Jamaican food and I greedily wolfed down my meal, not realising that these authentic flavours tantalizing my tongue would only be tasted again when I returned home to Jamaica. Finally, the announcement was made that we would be landing in thirty minutes. Even though this was the same airport I had flown in and out of for my first visit to London, I was utterly disoriented and overwhelmed when I disembarked from the place. In my anxious state, the airport seemed to have grown by miles since my visit a few months ago. My ears were blocked and I couldn't hear the announcements directing people to where customs was, and the entire ground I stood on felt unsteady. I thought maybe there was an earthquake starting, but realised that everyone else around me was moving with calm purpose.

I was surprised by the cold chill in the air, even though we were inside. It was certainly the wet chilly weather that London is famous for in the autumn that was sneaking into the building. I snapped out of my daze and tried to catch up with the other passengers from my flight, assuming the direction they were all going was the correct one. I knew it wasn't snowing outside this early at the end of the year, but all of the other passengers were retrieving heavy Jasmin coats from their luggage – I was not prepared for this at all. I joined the queue to clear customs and followed the instructions for those without UK citizenship; it was much longer than one for the British citizens. It was obvious that our flight was not the only one that had landed at this time. There was a great assortment of people in my queue; I took in the various shades of skin colour, all sorts of traditional clothing I had never seen before and the cacophony of strange languages. I was relieved to finally recognise some of my native people, a family who had travelled on the same flight I had been on, but I breathed a sharp intake of breath as they were gathered up by the stern authorities and taken away. I wondered what had they done because they didn't look suspicious to me at all and seemed much more relaxed than I was. I was struck with panic; would they come and detain me as well? I certainly looked like a worried nutcase. Another lady from the flight must have sensed my anxiety and confusion because she leaned over and whispered, "Drug mules." I was surprised at my ignorance but breathed a sigh of relief and realised that my hypersensitive state was more the norm for people legally immigrating to a new country.

I reached the customs window without incident. The officer hardly looked at me, simply stamping my passport and telling me in a bored voice to "Have a good day." I settled myself in the arrivals section of the airport. I was so anxious to call home and tell Tobore I had arrived safely and hear my daughter's sweet voice. But my Jamaica-based service was unable to pick up a signal and I realised I really was on my own.

"Sometimes it's best to be unsure of what lies ahead of us because if we knew, there wouldn't be any great adventure or ability or build resilience."

CHAPTER 9

"The unknown is sometimes started with excitement and anticipation that isn't realise at firs. It's then that we have to accept we weren't prepared for the unknown."

I had been told that a representative from the employment agency would meet me in the arrivals area of the airport, and take me to the home they had arranged for me to stay in while I settled into my new life and job. But as I looked around, I couldn't make out any particular person among the hundreds of people who were crowded, waving frantically to loved ones and rushing around to hug long-missed parents and lovers. To me, the room was cavernous and filled with laughing, chatting people whose lives had just been completed by the dear ones now in their arms.

On the edge of this melee were a few men standing sombrely and holding up placards with arriving passengers names printed on them. I was so relieved to realise that maybe one of these men might be from the agency and waiting patiently to collect me. I walked past each man in turn, carefully reading each card to find the one baring my name. When I reached the end of the line, I doubled back to look again, thinking I must have somehow missed the one with my name on it. But my second search was as fruitless as the first. I began to think that I may have landed at a different airport than they were expecting to pick me up at. I rechecked all of my notes from talking with the agency before I left. I even rechecked my boarding tickets which clearly read Heathrow Airport and when I asked an employee walking past, he confirmed that I had landed at the right place.

I began to think that the agency representative might simply be running late. I settled myself in a chair close to the area where the pick-up gathered for each arriving flight, so as not to miss my person when they arrived. After thirty minutes ticked by, I found another airport employee and explained my situation of just having arrived and finding no one to pick me up and having no service on my mobile. The employee directed me to a bank of public phones, but when I went to use one, I remembered that I had yet to exchange my Jamaican dollars for British pounds. Luckily, someone nearby noticed my plight and graciously handed me some coins and I immediately dialled the agency.

The woman who answered the phone was surprised to hear that I was waiting at the airport and admitted they had overlooked the fact that I was landing that day. I breathed a sigh of relief when she said to sit tight because they would send someone to come get me right away. In this case, however, 'right away' really meant another hour and a half and the representative I was expecting turned out to be a cab driver who barely spoke English. I felt a rush of camaraderie for this fellow immigrant, but soon understood that our conversation would be limited to monosyllabic words. The driver took me to a hotel and gestured for me to go inside and check-in while he waited with my luggage outside. When I went to the reception desk though I was told that there was no Ava Brown on their guest list. At first I assumed that the agency may have used a variation on the spelling of my full name that was causing confusion, but after the receptionist checked the guest list again with every possible variation of my name, she still came up with nothing. A sense of panic flooded over me; here I was in the middle of London, homeless, with nothing that the agency promised, when I could have been easing into my king-sized bed with the knowledge that my house-helper had taken care of all my family's needs.

When I expressed my predicament to the cab driver, he understood and made some calls back to the agency. As he was chattering away in a mix of English and some foreign language I didn't understand, I began to feel like I was a product being bartered in the human slave trade. I realised I was at the mercy of this agency that I had trusted to bring me to another country, owing them something already for getting my work permit; little did I know how the process worked, with the school that I would be working for paying thousands of pounds to the agency as a 'finder's fee'. The cab driver finally finished the call and told me that we were at the wrong hotel and he would take me to the right one.

We drove in pensive silence to the north of London and stopped in front of a tall building with the term 'hostel' in big white letters above the door. I had no idea what a hostel was, but I learned exactly how it was different from a hotel as soon as I entered it. The communal living atmosphere reminded me of the dorms I had lived in while at college. But, here I was, a woman with a husband a child and a successful career behind me; I was no longer a teenager who was comfortable sharing a single bathroom down the hall and noisy, tight-packed bedrooms.

This time, the cab driver brought my luggage inside and drove off after gesturing me towards the reception desk. This time, my name was on the guest list. I was given the key to my room and informed that I would be sharing a room with eight other people. I could hardly believe what I was hearing…eight other people? How could that be? Even when I lived in the cramped single-room house of my mother as a child, we didn't have nine people in it. My quick assessment of the lobby did not bode well and as expected, when I reached the living quarters, I found filth and chaos. The bathrooms looked like they hadn't been cleaned in years and there was a buzz of activity, with people of many different colours, race and languages jostling about the narrow hallways, in and out of our room.

In Jamaica, the language was either Patios or English, but here there was Russian, French, Italian and Polish. I soon realised that the many people of different origins were interacting as one group, and that made me feel even more of an outsider. In addition, I was keenly aware that I was the only black person and that made me feel even more isolated. "What have I gotten myself into?" I asked myself out loud, but either the people around me hadn't understood me, or they were just far too busy getting on with their own lives to care about this new addition to their already crowded home.

The room we all shared was about 14x15 meters with three-tiered bunk beds along the two side walls and two flat beds in the centre. There was absolutely no privacy. I had been assigned one of the bunk beds which was covered in the filth of an unknown amount of people who had slept on it before me. I envisioned myself in prison and couldn't believe that I had condemned myself to this sentence of suffering. I tucked my belongings in the small space that had been spared for me and went to bed that night in a state of complete disillusionment, crying into the disgusting pillow because I missed my home, my daughter and my husband. I felt so cheated and misled.

Settling into my new life in London quickly proved to be more emotionally difficult than I could have ever imagined. Every night as I lay down to sleep I lamented the life I had left behind in Jamaica, blinding myself to all of the difficulties I had endured and remembering only the good times and all of my successes. I berated myself for having left an excellent paying job, my friends and family. I would constantly cry myself to sleep thinking about how I had abandoned the simplest pleasures in life in my home country, like knocking on the neighbour's door just to say good morning or the ability to ask friends and family for a favour and being confident of the laid-back response being a kind "no problem irie mon" in our friendly sing-song accent. I consoled myself by remembering a piece of advice that my dear friend Dee had given me during a particularly difficult period of my life: God doesn't take us through dirty water to drown us, but to cleanse us.

I had arrived in London with nothing more than what had fit into my single piece of luggage, bringing minimal clothing and only what I thought would protect me against the intense, wet and cold weather I imagined existed year-round. Establishing my new life with these relatively few possessions was a daily reminder that I had consciously chosen to leave behind a lifestyle of luxury and certainty to start all over again. I felt as if I was back in the first week of college, the poor girl without the appropriate items to do my work and without any friends. However, the fear that still lurked in my heart about the men who had attacked me on that fateful night compelled me to reflect on the justifications I had given myself for moving to London in the first place. I reminded myself that Jamaica had once been a colony of England and of the significant influences on our culture that were still evident today. I told myself I was just being a silly girl. How different could the two countries really be?

My roommates seemed to be settled into the hostel lifestyle. But I found it very difficult to adjust, especially the lack of privacy and the requirement to share a toilet and a shower with so many strangers. The shower was on the third floor, and I had to take six flights of stairs to get there, carrying with me all of the toiletries I would need. I would wearily climb the stairs every morning; my arms loaded with my towel, toothbrush, soap, toothpaste, lotion, underwear, and most importantly bath slippers to protect myself from contracting the fungal skin diseases that were rampant among this community. I would also take my clothes to get dressed for the day, since the shower room provided the only privacy and I was incredibly uncomfortable with the sexually liberal attitude that I was seeing all around me.

The hostel provided meals for all of its residents, but I had an extremely hard time eating the daily dinner rations of bland mashed potatoes, runny brown gravy, and fatty English sausages. Sleep was never easy either and an undisturbed eight hours was impossible. I soon found out that my roommates worked all worked in different jobs. Some worked in the food service and others at the twenty-four hour cab dispatch offices. As such, we all kept different schedules and the lights in the room were going on and off at all hours of the night. It seemed as if we were all in a constant overlap of going-to-work and coming-home schedules, with someone coming in at dawn exhausted from the late night shift just when someone else was crawling out of bed, exhausted from lack of sleep to get dressed and head out to join the morning commute. It felt like I was living out a multitude of scenes in a movie all at once that was set in fast-forward.

Another difficulty in this living situation was the potpourri of smells that assaulted the nose throughout the day and night. I am sure that I smelled as strange to the others in the hostel as they did to me. We were such a mismatch of body odours that revealed our cultural beliefs of how much bathing is appropriate and what kind of foods are eaten in our nations. And, almost everyone sought out their native foods when they were outside of the hostel. The breakfast menu was not much better than the dinner menu, and just as unchanging.

The smell of eggs frying in stale oil permeated the entire building every morning as the sun rose. I would drag myself down to the breakfast area because if you missed breakfast, you were on your own until dinner, and when money was tight this was my only option for food that day.

The cleanliness of the dishes we ate from was equal to that of the rest of the hostel and the food was of very low quality. My first morning at the hostel, I looked down at my plate and imagined it shouting out "don't eat me! I am not clean!" The bread looked as if it had been obtained on sale after being rejected from the production line, the eggs were barely warm and runny, and the sausage was undercooked to the point of being nearly raw. My stomach knotted and I nearly gagged at the thought of eating this meal, but I knew I needed sustenance for the day ahead of me. My most important duty was to find a place where I could get my phone activated so that I could hear the voice of my sweet daughter and remember the reasons I must endure this situation – to create a safer life for her and I and to create a more stable home life for our family.

"Being in the wilderness without a familiar object is like being left to die, but faith will allow you to survive until rescue can come."

CHAPTER 10

"The mundane things in modern life, like technology, can be one's best friend in the desert."

I found a mobile phone shop about twenty metres from the hostel that sold SIM cards, which I hoped would allow me to access international calling on my phone. The price was steep, especially considering the very few pounds I had to survive off of until I started to receive my salary from the teaching job. I was incredibly hopeful as I handed over the non-refundable money and watched the salesperson insert the card into my phone. I was practically breathing down his neck as he held up the phone in the air and together we watched the screen as it searched for a signal. I laughed out loud with glee when the signal bars filled up to the highest range, showing strong connectivity. Finally, I was returning back to civilisation!

It was my second day in London and the agency had not left any message at the hostel. I checked to see if they may have been trying to contact me through my mobile phone, but there were no messages on it either. This was strange; prior to my arrival they had been in routine contact, constantly reassuring me that they would take care of me when I arrived in this new country. After the debacle at the airport, I couldn't imagine them forgetting me again so soon. I called the agency's main office, but only got a receptionist. She had no power but could only promise to pass on my message to an upper-level staff member. I left my mobile number and asked for a return call. My anxiety was again beginning to heighten. I thought in panic of how much I was at the mercy of these people who I had no reason to trust. I only had their word. Again, I thought of all the stories I had heard of unsuspecting immigrants landing in a county only to be placed in indentured servitude or outright slavery.

A tense two hours later, my mobile rang and I was greeted by the branch manager of the agency. His apologies for all the messy planning up to this point; I couldn't get in a word edge-wise. When he finished his jovial rant of promising that everything would be well from now on, I was finally able to express myself. And express myself I did! I let out all the disgust I felt about being treated as nothing more than an after-thought and the horrible living conditions in a barrage of complaints. He waited on the other end of the line in a patient silence, and then told me I needed to collect my belongings and find my way over to the office in south London to discuss the details of starting my job right away and to get settled into a better environment. I was still fuming, though, and yelled into the phone, "I am in the north right now! Don't you have an office nearby where you can put me to live?!" His reply was curt. He told me that I needed to find my way to their office, which was located on the south side of the city. He capped it off with a biting comment, "You said in your interview that you were a dedicated employee, who wasn't lazy."

I was so offended. I wanted to end the conversation right then by telling him to just fuck off. Instead, I bit my tongue and kicked the wall. We both knew the predicament that I needed his help due to the predicament I was in. I took a deep breath and thought to approach the situation like I would have with any cantankerous client in my old sales job. I kindly asked if the agency would send another cab to come and get me, but felt like I hit a wall when he snapped "I would imagine you can read and get yourself from point A to point B, you mentioned in our chat that you travelled to the US frequently, well it is the same to be fair just a different country. This is what working adults do, and I trust you are not a child. We don't employ children either." He cleverly placed a chuckle here to break the atmosphere.

I stood in stunned silence and then thought about how I was to accomplish this feat. I mumbled something about getting a cab, and he replied by telling me to have the cab drop me off in Mitcham town centre then to give him a call and he would provide me with the necessary walking directions from that point. At this point, he hung up and all of the frustration at the indignities he had thrown at me came boiling to the surface. I let out a giant scream and stomped like a two-year-old. The passers-by must have thought I was a mad woman!

I steeled myself for the travel to Mitcham town centre, wherever that was. I consoled myself with the thought that at least I would be leaving this disgusting hostel. However, when I went up to my room to gather my things, I found my bag lying open and broken on the floor. My things were strewn about and all the money I had brought was gone – thank God I had tucked some away in my purse and taken it with me when I left on my errands – along with the more expensive items of clothing and desirable personal care items. There was no way to know who had done this, as everyone had access to where the tenants' luggage was kept. My only recourse was to pack up what was left, improvise a quick fix to the latch so that it would be semi-functional, and check out.

I didn't know where I would be sleeping tonight, but I didn't even care at this point. As I dragged my broken bag outside of the hostel's front doors, I felt as if I was wearing all of its grim on my skin. A white man, who I recognised as one of the young immigrants from Kosovo that were living at the hostel, noticed my struggle and offered to help me. I almost wept at his simple gesture of kindness. I realised then that the cold personalities I had encountered so far in London were almost more than I could bear. In that moment, my heart ached so much for my home country that I thought it might break. Never in your wildest dreams would a Jamaican man stand by and ignore a female in need of physical help. The young man could see my turmoil, and without a word, he took the bag from me and carried it down to the curb side.

I didn't have to wait long for the cab that had been called by the front desk to arrive. I loaded my things into the back and directed the driver to Mitcham town centre. Before we set off, I asked him how much it would cost, but he said he couldn't say for certain as the cab fares are based on the mileage covered. All I knew was that London was large. I had no clue how far my destination was from this point, and I prayed that the money I still had in my purse was enough to cover the fare. My body and mind were so drained from the emotional turmoil of my first few days in London that the movement of the car lulled me into a deep sleep. I remember clearly how I dreamt about Jamaica, imagining that I was seated on a plane and on my way back home. I felt a gentle tap on my shoulder and smiled, thinking it was my baby Jasmin waking me up as she normally would do. But when I opened my eyes to see only the Rastafarian immigrant face of the cabbie, tears streamed from my eyes.

"Madam," he said, "we are in Mitcham". I was still very groggy and looked around; searching desperately for scenes that would tell me I was really alighting in Jamaica. But there was only the drizzly London weather and people tightly wrapped against the chill with their heads down and hands tucked firmly in their pockets as they stalked through the town square. The shock of this scene was too much and I started bawling outright. The driver was at a loss about what to do with me. He stepped away and instead busied himself with removing my luggage from the car and setting it carefully on the sidewalk. I finally gathered myself enough to ask him what the fare was - forty pounds. It would take nearly half of all the pounds I had in my wallet.

When I handed the money over, the cab driver asked me what was wrong. I shrugged off his question and told him that I was fine, but in a hurry to make an appointment. I did not want to air all of my complaints in the middle of this public street to a perfect stranger. Still, he placed an empathetic hand on my shoulder and told me to be strong. As he handed me a card with his number on it, he said "It all comes together at some stage. I meet new immigrants from the Caribbean all the time and they are always overwhelmed by this massive city. With time, it will get better." I felt like God had sent this angel to deliver just the right message to strengthen my resolve to continue to go forward.

I tucked his card in a safe place in my purse. I felt like I was no longer a complete stranger in this country, I now had met one person who was willing to offer the hand of friendship. As he got back into his cab, he gave me one last piece of advice, he told me the quicker I picked myself up, the better it would be for me because the path to my future in this new country was going to be rocky. And soon, I discovered that he was right on both of these points.

I finally snapped back to reality and made the call to the agency to tell my handler, whom I had begun to think of as my owner, I had arrived in the town centre. He asked me to tell him a landmark nearby my location and then told me that I was a short twenty-minute walk from where he was currently doing some business, which was closer than the office. When I arrived at the destination, I found the man was a tall white Briton. He formally introduced himself for the first time and I learned his name was James Tuckader; I could call him Mr. Tuckader. In an unexpected gesture of kindness, he said that he had driven near to the town centre to do some business and pick me up. The drive to the office in Clapham was completed in absolute silence, and this time I was much too anxious to fall asleep.

When we arrived, he directed me to a small room with a desk and quickly got down to the business of explaining the details of my employment, where I would be working, what hours I was expected to be there and whom I would be reporting to. Without any unnecessary pleasantries, he then took me back to his car and drove me to the school that I would be working in; a large public high school. We sat in the main reception area, on hard plastic chairs for a good forty five minutes. All that time there was a din of boisterous teenaged shouting and jostling in the surrounding corridors. I was utterly confused because the schools in Jamaica were so strict and the children were expected to be well behaved in all grades.

Finally, the door to one of the inner offices burst open and a thin, sallow-skinned white woman rushed in and made a beeline straight for us with a stern look on her face. She introduced herself as the deputy head teacher. Even though she was brisk and unfriendly, I was impressed with her efficiency. She spoke with us briefly and handed us over to the school's financial officer, who then surreptitiously handed an envelope to Mr. Tuckader. I assumed this was the agency's finder's fee that was paid for me and which made me really feel like I was being sold like a slave. I realised from my eavesdropping on their jovial yet argumentative conversation that the school was paying quite a tidy sum for me. The financier was an obese white woman, who wore a tent-like bright yellow floppy housecoat with frills and flapped her arms about when she spoke so that she looked like the giant talking bird character from a popular children's show back home. I did not realise then that this was her regular daily attire and that the students and staff alike secretly referred to her by the name of that very same character.

When the handing over and what I imagined to be the financial transaction was completed, she stood and shook hands with me, commenting on how smartly dressed I was for their humble school. I thanked her, but soon realised that it wasn't really the compliment I had assumed it to be. I was wearing one of my power suits, which I was so accustomed to wearing in my executive job in Jamaica to convey a sense of professionalism. I had thought this was appropriate because the teachers in Jamaica always dressed professional and modestly, with all unnecessary skin covered up and tattoos hidden. The concept back home is that teachers are supposed to be models for the students to emulate.

I had dressed in my suit out of respect for the teaching profession and for the children I would be mentoring. But as I started paying attention to the students and teachers who were going back and forth in the corridor, I realised that I was terribly overdressed. I lamented that fact that even the dress that made me feel successful and capable in Jamaica only made me feel awkward and uncomfortable in a first world country. I buried these feelings and held my head high as I was given the grand tour of the school. At the end, I felt totally lost in this new world and thought that I was intruding where I so clearly didn't belong. We passed classroom after classroom filled with screaming teenagers who were left on their own and were now jumping around the room. At first, I thought we must be in the drama department, where pupils were practicing for an upcoming play, but as the tour continued I realised that these were just regular classes and that the teachers simply had no control over their pupils. It was the students who 'roosted' this school, and the staff merely clucked around them. The tour guide must have noticed my surprise because she told me not to worry because this wild behaviour was only expected at the beginning and end of the school year, when the children are still hyperactive with the thought of the summer break.

The guide told us that the next stop would be the technology department of the school, where I would be working. She gave an embarrassed titter and admitted that the school was so large that even though she had been there for two years and was a senior manager, she didn't know where this block of classrooms was. I knew right there that my rocky path in England that the cab driver had predicted would not include only my personal life, but my professional one as well.

"Sometimes we end up in situations where running is our best option, but when we find that there is nowhere to run, we just stand."

CHAPTER 11

"Life can sometimes toss, shove and send you into the wilderness before it brings you back to civilization, the place you ideally want to be at."

The transition from being an employee in the private corporate sector, to becoming one in the state-run school system was a shock to say the least. In addition, the school's curriculum and teaching role was completely different than what I had been trained for in my home country. I was confused as to how could two countries that spoke a similar language and had a shared history could be so different? My fellow teachers and the school staff turned out to be very polite and eager to help me get settled in to my new teaching post, but I could not shake my homesickness and the feeling of culture shock. I struggled to overcome my subdued mood and match the enthusiasm of my colleagues, but my smiles never reached my eyes and belied my belief in the Jamaican proverb to be weary of overly friendly people.

My general disorientation in this new setting only strengthened my paranoia that had been born on the night I was attacked. I remained on high alert in any situation involving strangers, including all of my colleagues and pupils. My inability to form any bonds within this social group pushed me deeper into a depression. For the first week, I would start each day in my classroom by arriving early, before the students, so that I could gather myself for being an effective instructor. Inevitably, as I would look around the empty room filled with desks, my resolve would crumble and I would sink into a ten-minute sob fest. My crying was so intense in these days that I would hear myself gasping for breath and moaning out loud. I remember the horror that would strike my heart when I would hear myself and it would make me cry harder. I also worried about what my colleagues would think if they heard me, so I would bury my head in my handbag to suffocate the noises of deep emotional pain that were escaping from within me.

I could not escape my misery. I wanted to be gone from this strange place where I did not fit in. I wanted to be back at home with my daughter and my husband by my side. I wanted the past year to have been only a bad dream. I began to convince myself that the threats to my life were not real after all, that I had somehow misunderstood my attackers parting words or dreamed their second visit to my home. I was desperate to return to the familiar world that I now felt foolish to have fled. There were so few black people in this new town and my uniquely dark skin colour for this region made me feel even more isolated. I yearned for the days when I could have simply walked around my local community and find any number of extended family members to complain to or commiserate with. Here, I didn't even get a simple good morning from passers-by on the street. I even began to miss the distant and sometimes tenuous relationships that I had with my mum and siblings.

On my first day at the school, the man from the agency had excused himself shortly after my tour of the building had begun. As he tried to sneak off, I grabbed him by the jacket so that he wouldn't get away without telling me where I was to be staying that night; after all, I had checked out of the hostel and my luggage was still in his car. He told me that he would drop my bag off in the school's main office and I could find it there at the end of the day. For the second time today, I found out that it would be up to me to take care of myself.

When the tour ended, the ladies in the school's main office were kind enough to make some calls to various B&Bs in the area. After several calls, they found one with a vacancy in the south of London. When the secretary asked me to approve the price of twenty pounds per night so that she could make my reservation, I agreed with trepidation in my heart – twenty pounds was almost the exact amount of money I had left in my wallet. The secretary also provided me with the bus schedule, so that I could catch a ride directly from the front of the school to my new lodgings. The bus was crowded with people travelling home from the end of the workday across the city, and in the entire hubbub, I missed my stop. I was relieved to find that the next stop was only a five minute walk from the one where I should have gotten off.

I found the B&B rather easily and felt like my luck was finally changing. This building was a paradise compared to the hostel. As I approached the shining oaken reception desk, I wondered just what would have happened if I had had no money left to pay for this? I shuddered to think that the agency would have just abandoned me to sleep on the street at this point - with their commission in hand there was no need to concern themselves with me anymore. The receptionist took my money as prepayment for the night and informed me that there was no access to a phone line. I smiled, because for once today, a challenge was not insurmountable; my phone was still showing a strong signal and I would be able to call home as soon as I got settled.

The collective cost of my taxi fare, the bus fare and the lodging fee left me nearly broke. I had no money for a proper meal before bed that night, so I focused my energies on taking a much needed shower in the B&Bs clean bathroom and then found a small shop where I could purchase a loaf of sliced bread and a two-litre cream soda, which were to serve as my dinner for as long as it took for me to get some money wired from my account in Jamaica, or for my first paycheque to come. I retired to the privacy of my well-kept room at the B&B and picked at the inadequate meal. In Jamaica, I was accustomed to a hearty dinner each night, which would include everything from oxtail, rice and peas, coleslaw and potato salad, to fried chicken, bacon, and eggs; my help had been a lavish cook! My new life in England was so different from that in Jamaica that I felt as if I had been transported to another world and not just another country.

Having that little bit of bread and soda in my stomach fortified my spirit more so than it did my physical state. Despite my situation being nothing as I had imagined it to be, I recalled my natural strength of perseverance. I resolved to make this move work no matter what by reminding myself of the fact that my daughter and sister were coming to join me here in October. There was no way I was going to allow them to arrive to find the same frightening uncertainty that I had.

When I drifted off to sleep that night, I had serene dreams filled with my daughter's sweet laughter and the sensation of her little arms hugging me. Before I knew it, the alarm was jolting me awake, alerting me to the impending workday ahead of me. I had slept so deeply that I was disoriented by my surroundings for a few moments. Finally, the realisation that I was in London, about to start teaching at the high school and needing to check out of the B&B crept into my mind. I took another long shower, luxuriating in the extreme cleanliness of this bathroom compared to that of the hostel. As the hot water cascaded over my head, covering my body like a blanket, my brain and soul woke up and I steeled myself to handle all of the new challenges that lay ahead of me that day. The B&B served a hot and hearty breakfast and I ate as much as my stomach could hold, knowing that my next meals would only consist of the leftover bread and soda that was now tucked among my belongings in my luggage.

Even though my heart was aching to hear the voices of my daughter, my sister and Tobore, I hesitated to call them with only complaints about my first few days in the place that was soon to be their new home. Instead, I placed a call to a childhood friend, Jos, who offered to provide me with a quick loan of British pounds so that I could rent a place before my financial matters were settled. Since I was expected to be at work all day, I would have to use the evening to look for a place to live permanently. I hoped I would find something immediately, and not have to return to the B&B again, as night-by-night lodging is always more expensive than a monthly rental. I borrowed a local newspaper from the reception desk and scanned the advertisements as I finished my breakfast.

Without thinking, I immediately started to seek out houses that matched what we had in Jamaica, but the exorbitant rates that were published next to each, quickly jolted me into reality; there was no way I would be able to afford a dwelling large enough for each of us to have separate rooms and extra space for socialising. I scanned the adverts until I reached the section at the end that was more 'poor man's housing' and I took a sharp intake of breath when I realised that even these prices were incredibly high by Jamaican standards. In all my considerations about accepting the teaching job in London, it never occurred to me to consider the drastic difference in cost of living, which reduced my already low pay to nearly nothing. I cursed myself for having made such a rash decision to immigrate; clearly, I had not thought this through adequately.

I caught the bus to work and was again overwhelmed by the newness of my surroundings. The buildings were tall and crowded together. Everything looked the same to me, including the people on the streets, who all wore dour expressions and kept to themselves. When I arrived in my classroom that morning, I met the first of my students. The informal interactions between pupils and teachers struck me as it had the day before. I planned to overcome this and establish a sense of decorum in my classroom by instructing my students to take their seats and give me their attention while I gave a very formal introduction about myself.

I stood straight up in front of the class and gave a proper oration about who I was, where I was from and what my hopes were in regards to helping guide their lives and enriching their education. I asked the pupils to introduce themselves one-by-one. When we got to one boy who was of Caribbean descent, he concluded his introduction by saying to me, "hey, I have seen you somewhere before". I immediately labelled this boy as the class clown, and I was more than ready to put a stop to this attention-seeking behaviour. I brushed his comment off with ease, but was thrown off balance when the boy stood up and pointed at me and exclaimed, "Oh yes! I have seen you before, in the paper! My mum and dad just came back from the big reggae show in Jamaica, and you were in the paper they brought back". I laughed his words off, but that just riled him more. He looked me straight in the eye and said, "I will bring that paper tomorrow and prove you wrong". He was so emphatic that I agreed that he should bring the paper in so that I could see myself in print.

Turns out, he was right. When he came in the next day with the paper, there I was staring out from the front page, dressed to the nines at one of the last big galas I had attended for the telecom company. The fact that I was standing next to a singer who was very popular worldwide at the time impressed my students and gave me a bit of respect in their eyes. I silently thanked God that this was the story in which I was headlining, and not a report of the brutal crime that I had just survived.

The resources at this new school were nothing like I have ever seen before. I felt like the students were being educated in the lap of luxury. Back at my high school in Jamaica, we had learned about photosynthesis by picking leaves off of trees outside and holding them up to the sun to squint at the structures that the bright light made semi-translucent. This school was full of the latest technology and clever exaggerated representations of even the smallest of molecules and elements. Even though these resources were advanced, I lamented that as a teacher here, I wouldn't have the ability to teach the children the important life lesson of improvising and using your creativity to overcome a challenge.

My strict demeanour allowed me to gain some semblance of control over the pupils in my classroom, but on the whole, my impression from the first day in the school was correct and most of the other classrooms seemed completely out of control. I found out that the lower grade feeder schools for this high school were all same-sex schools, so for many students, this was their first experience of attending with the opposite sex. The titillation that these students felt at being in a co-ed structure meant that many teachers were merely policing the hormone-driven students rather than teaching them. I noticed the sexual tension even in my own classroom, which was visible in the way that the children sat themselves on opposite sides of the room according to gender. I would laugh inwardly because sometimes the room would look like a community ruled by two rival gangs who had no trust of each other.

I made a concerted effort to help the girls and boys begin to interact with one another more naturally by formally assigning seating that mixed up the two. This arrangement was met with much loud grumbling, but I overruled it all and the classroom benefited from it in the end. Sooner than I had dared to hope, I found my footing in the classroom and the lessons started becoming interesting for the students. I did make an attempt to instil the importance of smart dressing, but that was largely a failure. The style for boys at the time was to wear their trousers down past their hips, so that their ass was literally hanging out, covered by thin cotton boxer shorts with wild prints on them. It was also the style to look a bit grungy, but boys of that age need to bathe and they often smelled rather 'ripe' from their boisterous activities.

I was continually surprised when the students would show up completely unprepared for lessons, carrying no pens, pencils or books. There was a particular group of boys and girls who were already quite hardened to life and who accepted no amount of guidance. The boys would almost always skip class, and instead wander the corridors in search of their own entertainment. Unfortunately, that entertainment consisted of accosting anyone they found alone and this even included the staff and teachers who they harassed relentlessly because they knew that the law would favour them if they made any false accusation of abuse. I soon found that I was not immune to their torments. On one particular occasion, one of the rougher girls in this gang shoved me up against a window and threatened to thrust me straight through the glass in retaliation for my having reprimanded her during class. When I made a complaint to the administration, I was told there was no recourse since it had happened without any witnesses besides her group of friends, who they assured me, would lie for her.

My personal living situation got settled pretty quickly. I found a small flat to rent in a multi-storied building in an ideal location. It was near the train station and bus depot as well as several fruiters and banks. The floor plan consisted of a front social room (which also served as a second bedroom), a proper bedroom, kitchen and bathroom. My flat was on the ground floor, and the flat below ground level was occupied by a number of African men living together in a place of similar design and size. The men, though, packed in together and sometimes rowdy, were courteous whenever we met, but I was still very fearful of strange men, especially when they were in groups, so I always kept a far distance.

While the place was cramped and dingy, it served my purpose. I dismissed my disappointment by reminding myself that this flat was simply a stop-gap along the journey to my great life in London. Still, I greatly missed all the luxuries of the home I had abandoned back in Jamaica and I began to worry about what my family would be expecting to live in when they finally arrived. Would they condemn me as a failure when they found no king size bed with Egyptian cotton sheets, ensuite bathroom, or walk in closet?

When I moved in, I got a better appreciation for just how dirty the last tenants had left the place. The carpets were thoroughly soiled and there was a prevalent underlying odour of mould that began to cling to everything I owned. I had no money to clean it, but I was also working so many extended hours at the school that I had no time to care about it. I had also managed to make a friend from among my colleagues at the school, another young teacher named Soha who immediately proved herself a trustworthy confidant. It was she who recognised that the struggle with my finances could be resolved by getting a flatmate to share the cost of rent. My first reaction to her recommendation was horror. Without thinking, I argued that it was impossible. I was a woman, I was a mother and a wife, I owned my own luxurious home back in Jamaica; communal living is for youngsters who are just starting out, I stated flatly. She simply looked me straight in the eye and asked me if I had really just described myself. She also explained that she knew that the agency wouldn't be paying up front, so I would need to wait some time for my first pay cheque, and that it often took longer than expected to get international banking matters resolved.

I was utterly frustrated to realise that she was right. I had very little money left from the loan I had taken from my other friend. Really, I had no choice but to get a flat mate, if I was going to be able to stay in the dirty little hovel I had managed to acquire. I put out an advert in the free local paper, but had little time to devote to vetting interested parties. Ultimately, I accepted the first person who turned up in person and who agreed to pay the amount I asked for. If I had been thinking straight, I would have realised right away that this person was not someone I would have chosen to live with under any other circumstances. But, I was in London, the great equaliser, but I didn't have a lot of choice.

My flat-mate had grown up in the local ghetto, much like I had, but the similarities ended there. Where I spent my days and nights tirelessly working to improve my situation, she sat around primping for social outings. Her mass of bleaching creams, coloured wigs and scanty outfits took up a large portion of the front room. She was up at all hours of the night and would frequently return loudly from a boisterous night out in the wee hours of the morning which affected my sleep made settling into my new work routine a challenge. I made a mental note that professionals must flat share with like-minded professionals. Much like a marriage, a successful union of flat-mates relies on compatibility in the majority of things.

The situation with my flat-mate could not last, and I realised that the flat itself was absolutely unsuitable for my arriving family. I had settled into my role at the school and started to feel confident with the town itself, so I started looking for a new place where my daughter and sister could move into with me. They were expected to arrive in less than two months.

In the meantime, I began readying the dingy flat for the possibility of our needing to live there - minus the flatmate of course. I missed my daughter immensely, so getting the house prepared for her made me happy in a way that nothing else had since my arrival. There wasn't a great deal I could do with the flat, but I began to clean as much as possible, like a new mother who was nesting before the birth of their baby. I freshened up the foul carpet, obtained a nice, but cheap duvet cover and soft plush toys. I even sought out ethnic food shops to gather some familiar foods, to help ease Jasmin's and my sister's introduction to this new life. I learnt where the libraries, parks, schools, and churches were located.

As my excitement mounted, October seemed to approach at the pace of a snail. I began calling home frequently and spending all of my extra money on phone cards. Finally, the day arrived when they would land at Heathrow and there was no way I was going to let them experience the isolation and uncertainty I had when my flight had landed. The trip to the airport felt like I was driving across the country, instead of just across town. In my anxiousness, I managed to arrive at the airport several hours early, but I didn't care. I was just thrilled to finally be reunited with my baby girl.

After their flight had landed, the arrivals area became thick with people awaiting their loved ones to alight from the interior. I couldn't see past the crowds and was afraid I would miss Jasmin and my sister. As I craned my neck to look above the mass of people ahead of me, I heard an all too familiar voice saying, "Excuse me, has anyone seen my mum? Where is my mum?" I flew through the crowd and towards that little angelic voice of my daughter. There she was, such a big girl, confidently walking into the arrivals area, decked out in her denim jacket and matching jeans and a dainty pink bow laced through her hair. I flung my arms open wide and she landed in them like a little angel settling onto a cloud. We hugged in a deep, long embrace and I felt complete. Suddenly, it didn't matter how much I disliked this massive city and its strange culture, my life was filled with sunshine because my daughter was back with me.

I next grabbed my sister in a strong embrace and we headed out to face the challenges that London had to offer together. On the ride to our flat, I could see the looks of amazement and trepidation on their faces as they scanned the city outside of the cab windows. I was reminded of my first day here and I became even more determined to ensure that their experience would be easier than mine had been. They told me all about the flight and the newness of all they experienced while crossing the Atlantic. I told them about my job and the town in which we would be living in. The chattering continued when we got to the flat. My sister updated me on all the community news I had missed since September. We stayed up so late into the night that the cold began to creep in from the outside. Even though I had the front room cleared and set up for my sister to live in, we all snuggled in my bed together and fell asleep.

Neither Jasmin nor my sister cared or maybe even realises the poor state of the flat or the neighbourhood in which we were staying. Even though it met none of the high standards I had made them accustomed to back in Jamaica, they showed me that the only thing that mattered was that we were together. As I drifted off to sleep that night, happier and more fulfilled than I thought possible, I began to think about the next big thing we needed to prepare for. Tobore was coming in December.

"The presence, support and comfort of family is the best remedy for the soul."

CHAPTER 12

"Readjustments can sometimes feel like a crisis on self-esteem."

The adjustment of us all living together in the small flat took some time. I managed to get Jasmin registered in the neighbourhood school and helped Kem to find a job nearby which was literally a two-minute walk from our home. I was pleased to see how quickly these two girls were acclimatising and it served to inspire me in the same vein. Certainly, just having my two beloved family members by my side made London feel less like an island of banishment and more like our home. Even though I was still working long hours at the school, I took odd jobs to get the extra income we would need to be able to afford an adequately sized place that would accommodate the three of us as well as my husband when he arrived in December.

I was excited about Tobore's arrival, but also somewhat apprehensive. I felt we were strong enough individuals to overcome all of the hurt that had passed between us and mend the frayed connection. My prayers were that our relationship would work out since we would be leaving our major problems back in Jamaica. In fact, I believed we had already forgiven each other for all of our past transgressions and now we were ready to move on. Accepting the reality of his other child and suppressing my sense of utter betrayal had been hard, but knowing that he was sitting at home equally excited about coming to join me eased my pain.

As December rushed forward, I became more comfortable making the types of phone calls to just simply say "I miss you". On one morning when I had quickly finished getting ready for work and had a few extra minutes, I ducked into one of those iconic red

Ava Brown

telephone boxes and made such a call even though it was two a.m. in Montego Bay. I still remember the smile that was on my face as I held the phone to my ear, waiting to hear the sleepy voice of the man who had recaptured my heart. But to my surprise his friend answered the phone, telling me that Tobore had gone out for a walk and had left his phone behind. Something in his tone piqued my women's intuition and I knew I was being lied to. After all, I knew my husband well enough to know that he did not have the dreamy spirit of a poet who goes for contemplative walks on the beach in the middle of the night.

As I hung up, my mind immediately went to the memory of the day before I left for London, when his 'baby mama' was beating at his front door and screaming in heartbroken anguish. My fingers moved over the phone's number pad without me consciously moving them to dial her number. She answered on the third ring and my number must have shown on her screen because she simply said "Babe, it's for you" as she handed Tobore the phone.

To be perfectly honest I don't recall exactly what else transpired on the phone call after that moment. I do, however, remember how I physically felt all of the hope I had for our relationship waft up and out of my body, like steam rising from a hot 'cuppa'. All the dreams I carried inside my heart, that had buoyed me through the past months, disappeared into nothingness. Blackness started to close in around me and I nearly passed out, the phone slipping from my grasp and clanging sharply on a glass pane of the telephone box enclosure. I managed to keep myself upright and to stagger out of the phone booth and make my way to my school for the workday, crying the entire walk.

My mind was spinning. How could Tobore do this to me, to us, right after we had agreed to start over?

155

How could he so blatantly disrespect all of the hard work I was doing here to set up our new life and to ensure that his own transition would be easier than mine had been? The night we spent together before I left, we had made a solemn promise to one another, recommitting ourselves to the marriage vows that we had taken so many years before. He broke that promise. I was so distraught that when I arrived at work that I didn't care what the kids did that day. I allowed most of my classes to get up to their own thing. I sat at my desk in a near comatose state, staring at the floor and trying to not dissolve into tears. I couldn't be happier when the day finally ended.

Back at home that night, I didn't eat or speak to anyone. I just wanted to shut the world out. I reviewed all of the conversations that Tobore and I had shared since my arrival in London, searching desperately for any clue as to his true intentions; anything that I may have blinded myself to. Eventually, I called a friend back home in Jamaica, needing to unload this misery and find some support, but the conversation only led to my learning that Tobore had gone back to his lover's bed the day after my flight left.

Even though I was disgusted at the thought of Tobore coming to join us, I continued to look for a house that would fit our family. In November, I located a two-bedroom maisonette that was tiny, but a vast improvement over our dingy little flat. There was a garden in the back and a charming corner bathroom directly after the kitchen. I never could get used to the English design of putting the toilet beside the kitchen, but until I could afford to design my own home, I would have to live with the style that was normal in this country. In fact, many things that were normal fixtures in a middle-class home in Jamaica were considered amenities accompanied by a premium price in London, including the ensuite bathroom, a power-shower (which sometimes simply meant a shower head), a garden, dedicated or merely convenient parking, double glazed panelling and central heating.

The perception of England back in its previous colony, and a largely poor one, was that the motherland had streets paved with gold. While my expectations upon arrival were not quite so luxuriant, they were certainly higher than what I had been exposed to so far. I came to realise the importance of how things appear when one is on holiday and how they actually are for the full-time working citizens. Despite all of my petty complaints, the maisonette was the best that my budget could afford.

My sister, Jasmin and I moved in and we instantly fell in love with our new clean place. We were crammed but cosy. In addition, despite what had transpired between Tobore, I and his lover, he had told me that he was still planning to join us. I began to dread what was in store for us. We were soon to be back in the situation of enduring each other's company in a broken relationship with no hope of survival.

December arrived before I knew it and I found myself in a cab on the way to the airport to pick him up. I was surprised to find that a part of me was still happy to know that he was finally arriving after all this time. Maybe Jasmin's excitement at her daddy's arrival had rubbed off on me? Jasmin and my sister joined me on the trip to the airport and, to a stranger's eyes, we made a very joyous welcoming party. The journey home was more subdued and reflected the true feelings, or lack thereof, between my husband and I. It was clear on even that first night that mending our broken relationship was not going to work.

Over the next six months we made a somewhat valiant effort to rekindle our unconditional love for one another, but all of our interactions were tainted with the mistrust of the past. At the time, I did try to identify exactly what our fundamental problems were, so that we could attack them head on, but looking back I realise I was too close to the situation to be able to carry out this kind of self-investigation in a productive manner. The clarity of hindsight, supported by the years in between in which I have matured, has allowed me to see now what my faults were in the crumbling of our marriage.

I suffered greatly from low self-esteem, which had been further weakened by my experience with the attackers that had caused me to flee Jamaica in the first place. I had always felt inadequate next to Tobore, him being from such a strong and wealthy family compared to my own, but now I felt somewhat unworthy of him. I was plagued by the feeling that I had failed as a wife, blaming myself for his straying into the arms of another woman and creating another child. I felt that I was failing him even now, being the spouse that moved him from our luxurious life into this struggle for survival in a strange country, without our families or life-long friends.

We endured this tense life under the same roof for about six months, with no progress being made towards each other. Then one night, during the last weeks of the spring term at my school, our frustrations with one another came pouring out in a massive argument. At the end we were both physically and emotionally exhausted and I knew we could not go on like this without utterly destroying ourselves. In the silence that followed, I was the first to speak, "I will move out of the flat".

Within a few short days, I had secured another two-bedroom flat and moved myself, my sister and Jasmin into it. I had settled Jasmin and myself into one of the two bedrooms, so that Kem could have a room to herself. However, as our move-in day progressed, Kem never showed up after removing her things from the flat we were vacating. As the afternoon wore on, and I had no contact from her, I began to get nervous. "Oh, god, please don't let this be Jamaica all over again", I pleaded in silent prayer. I certainly did not have the income now to support her not coming to live with us and share in the expensive rent on a whim. I calmed myself by rerunning all of the conversations we had had in the previous days, when she constantly assured me she would stay with us and helped to pick out something we could afford on a two-person income.

As the evening began to fall, Kem finally called. My heart sank when I listened to her telling me that she had decided at the last minute to move in with her friend instead of Jasmin and me. I felt her words as if they were a slap to my face. I reasoned with her about the rental contract that I had signed, with the agreement that she was to live with us. Her answer was only to suggest that I abandon the new flat and find another that was smaller and which I could afford without her. When I explained again that this was impossible because I would lose all of the money I had deposited, but she was unmoved.

If I broke the rental agreement, I would have no money for a deposit on another place, so I went ahead and stayed in the flat with the knowledge that I had to find a flatmate, and quick! Luckily, the advert I put out in the next day's paper was answered promptly by a lovely white girl from Yorkshire, named Jenna. Before we knew it, she moved in and I finally felt some relief from my financial worries. Jenna wasn't the cleanest person, but she tried. She was kind-hearted and would try to help out as much as she was able to. For example, she would wash her dishes, but she never remembered to rinse the soap off them. I would have to go back and re-rinse anything in the cabinets so that Jasmin and I wouldn't get sick from eating the soap residue. She never thought to clean the bathroom, and I often felt like I was cleaning up after two children in my spare time. I began to picture myself as a child, doing endless chores every waking hour when not in the classroom, and I became convinced that my lot in life was to clean up after others. Still, I couldn't complain because she was always on time with her rent cheque.

When the Jasmin season rolled around that year, it blew Kem onto our doorstep, asking to move in with us. Jenna was still occupying the second bedroom and paying her part of the rent, so there was no room even if I had wanted to forgive my sister so quickly. I told her that I could not make the flat-mate vacate the house and explained that there was no room and that it would be terribly inappropriate of me to cram another person in the single bedroom that Jasmin and I shared.

Not surprisingly, Kem was quite upset with me. She cried and said that she was in need, that I was her blood, that she had come to rely on me as her fortress of protection when the world was not treating her kindly. It pained me to see this, but I had no option at this time. I had to harden my heart and realise the truth in what everyone else had always warned me of; I was a softie when it came to my sister and she preyed on me to make her life easier. Still, I could not just absolutely turn her away. I told her that I would help her find someone else who could help her out and provide a temporary or even a permanent place for her to stay.

Tobore had recently moved out of the flat we had rented together and I had helped him to find another place to rent through the woman who owned the house. Even though their situation was cramped, I thought that they may be able to accommodate one more person. I made the call and within thirty minutes the whole situation was resolved and Kem had somewhere she could live temporarily.

This stressful situation made me reflect on the freedom that came with owning one's own home. I missed having my own place terribly. The move to London had proved regressive in so many ways. I had stepped backwards in my career and was living more like a college student than as a woman who was a mother and provider. I decided that I needed to get my life together and focus on buying my own place. I knew I would have to rely on my traits of perseverance and determination to make this dream come true. I mentioned this new plan in passing conversations to some of my friends and was told to calm down because I was being too ambitious for my own good. "After all," they said, "you have only just come to Britain in the past year and so many others have been here for years and years and they still cannot buy a house." I didn't know anything about these other people, so I began planning how to make this idea work out.

"Perseverance can be the platform on which goodness is staged."

Chapter 13

"The most significant weapon people can use against us is playing with our minds."

It was a shock to find out at the end of the school year that my salary had not been divided on a twelve-month schedule and that any staff provided through the agency was not provided work in the summer holidays. I also found out that I was still considered a temporary worker (known as a 'supply teacher' provided by an employment agency), someone who they could choose to not extend on contract for the next school year. I understood why the agency had decided to hide this fact, because who in their right mind would give up their whole life and journey over four thousand five hundred miles to take an unstable job that could be revoked after only a few months? I began to panic when I thought about how I was going to be able to afford our monthly rent, and I lamented that I would never be able to save up to make my dream of purchasing a home a reality.

I was anxious to prove myself to the school in any way possible so that they would see what a good worker I was. I needed them to consider me an indispensable part of their teaching staff who should be hired on a permanent basis with a salary increase. I took on all sorts of extra duties and never said no to any requests that were asked of me. This was difficult since I also needed to be taking on other jobs in my spare time for additional income so I could save up to either provide for the months in the summer when I would be unemployed, or so that I could put into the savings for a down payment on a house.

Because of all the extra duties I was doing at the school, I had made a request of the deputy head teacher to please consider an increase in my salary, which was lower than that of the staff teachers. Instead of getting a response to my request, I was told by the head of faculty that I had been assigned to run an after school club in addition to all the other things I was doing on a voluntary basis. I didn't argue and instead called the agency to see if they had heard anything about my status at the school or whether an increase in my salary was at a negotiation stage. The answer was a resolute, "no, we haven't heard from the school at all in the past five months".

Since it appeared that nothing was going to get done without me pushing it forward, I scheduled a meeting with the head of faculty to discuss the disproportionate level of my workload and compensation. When we met, I was ready to use the extra club assignment as a bargaining chip in my negotiations, but she quickly shot that idea down. I was told that although clubs are technically voluntary, I wasn't employed in a position that allowed me to turn it down and that it was being assigned to me. She ended by firmly stating, "This is the role of the Food Technology teacher". I was absolutely frustrated! Even though I didn't mind running a club for the students, it was so unfair that I was expected to take it on without any consideration for my desire or time.

Unfortunately, the head of faculty was right; I wasn't in any position to deny this assignment or bargain for something better. They had me over a barrel. I had to accept whatever situation they put me in – regardless of the blatant unfairness of my doing equal or more work than the permanent staff while getting paid much less as a supply teacher – because my work permit was tied to this school. My conversation with the head of staff had left me far too timid to do fight back and potentially lose everything I had worked so hard for this far.

During my short time at the school, I had already seen numerous other supply teachers come and go. Since I was so busy and their tenures so short, I was never able to become friends with any of them and ask how they planned to survive the summer break with no pay. I started thinking about what other type of job I might be able to find for the six-week period, but remembered that my visa had a stipulation that forbade both work for any other entity besides the agency that brought me in and recourse to public funds.

With this realisation, I gathered up my courage and went to the head teacher to ask if there was any way that the school could pay me a retainer fee for the summer holidays, to make up for the absolute lack of income I was to have during that time. I was disappointed, but not surprised when she told me no. I called the agency again to find out if there was anything I could do to avoid the situation of financial stress that was impending, but was told that these terms had been explained to me before I arrived. I was in no position to argue this, as I had been in such a fragile mental state when I had accepted the job. For all I knew, they had detailed every last bit of this policy and I had simply not understood it. I didn't blame myself too much, after all, I would have never imagined that anyone would have set up a system in which they expect people to stay tied to an employer who does not provide any work for a part of the year, and then to restrict the employee's ability to do anything else gainful during this off period.

The one good thing about my job at the school was that the official workday ended at half-past two, so I could dash off to pick up my daughter at the end of her school day, even if I had other after school duties to attend to later in the day. I focused on this fact and decided not to let myself get depressed about the other things that were out of my control. Before I knew it, summer was upon us, and I had not been invited to work through the summer session at the school. I knew these next six weeks were going to be tough, and I prayed that God would bring us a miracle by stretching the little bit of money I had managed to save so that we could eat and keep a roof over our heads.

The time off passed relatively quickly and I returned back to work on the first day of the autumn term. Things progressed without incident and I was saving every penny that came into my hands. Before I knew it, I had saved up enough to start looking for a small house in the area that I could afford to buy. I found one and was thrilled to start the process of securing a mortgage.

As that part of my life began to come together, my life at work started to unravel. A tension had grown between the head teacher and myself, stemming from the disagreements we had at the end of the spring term. I wouldn't have minded if this tension remained unspoken, but I started to notice that the head was acting upon her displeasure with me. Several other employees who were much newer to the department than I was were suddenly offered promotions and I was completely unaware of the process by which they were selected for this honour. This baffled me, especially because I had been designated as a form teacher – this was a teacher who performed with excellence and was given newly qualified teachers (known as NQTs) to shadow them in order to learn the job. I loved being a form teacher and I was quickly assigned many NQTs because I was able to form such great relationships with my students.

However, before I could use this as an argument to support my request for a similar promotion, there was an unfortunate and unfair incident that occurred involving a boy in my class who had HIV and me falling on my sword. The boy's infection status was strictly confidential, and as far as I knew the NQTs were not privy to this information. Because of that policy, I never spoke to my newest NQT about the sensitivity of this information or provided her guidance in how to handle it. By the end of her first week I found out that she had told the entire NQT group of this boy's illness, and I was furious! I spoke to her in private at that time about the issue, but I could not calm down over her immaturity and the injustice that had been done by it.

My disappointment and anger did not subside and it showed itself in my interactions with her. In the end, I was called up by my supervisor and dressed down for my behaviour towards the NQT. I didn't want to make the situation worse than it was, so I didn't explain why I was so angry with her, as her original behaviour would have cost her job and ruined her entrance into a teaching career. I took full responsibility for my behaviour towards the NQT and remained quiet on everything else. The meeting was also attended by the assistant deputy head teacher, a fellow Jamaican who had immigrated many years before and who had abandoned all traces of her heritage. As the meeting ended, and I sat contrite in my chair with my head held low, she gave a single comment. Her biting advice to me was to get rid of the Jamaican attitude I carried with me, thinking that I was better than others.

This situation threw me over the edge; I no longer wanted to work under these conditions. I went home that evening and called the immigration department, just to enquire how I could apply for my own visa. I knew doing so was risky, as I would certainly be flagged as a visitor with questionable intent. The

Ava Brown

immigration representative told me the steps involved, but also warned me that there were no guarantees and that my application may in fact damage my future plans related to my current status. She explained that by starting the process, I would lose the four years that had been granted in the original visa, and my stay would be valid for only one year. I didn't care at this point and just wanted out of the bind I was in with this job that felt like indentured servitude.

Starting the process required that I asked my current employer for a reference. This would be tricky as it would alert them to my wanting to leave their employment, and I was worried they wouldn't let me go as I was basically cheap labour. I decided to tell them that I was requesting the reference for continuing my studies to get a bachelor's of business administration degree. In the end, this deceit actually worked in my favour, without my planning it, because I found out that my original degree wasn't accredited and I had to get another degree that the British regulatory bodies would recognise.

My real plan, however, was to take the letter of recommendation to the home office to apply for my own visa. I filled out the application for the 'highly skilled' visa, and my stay time was immediately reduced to one year. When I told my friends and family, the only response was that I must be mad. They asked why I had decided to limit myself to one year when I was struggling enough with the ability to try to make a successful go of this move in four. I, on the other hand, felt like a slave that had just been freed.

The next day, I went to the head of faculty and told her I was thinking of resigning. She sat back and looked at me with an emotionless expression on her face. She advised me in a cool voice to seriously consider my immigration status before I make any decisions. I told her that, as a matter of fact, I already had considered it and I had found a way where it wouldn't be a problem. She made no reply but merely raised her eyebrow in curiosity, her mouth turned down in a hint of displeasure. I could suddenly see my situation with clarity. I knew that the visa status was a way of holding workers like myself as prisoners. I felt confident of my decision to get out before it destroyed me.

I went home feeling rather chuffed with myself, knowing I had gotten the best of my jailers. I knew this was ego, but I didn't care. I was so proud of myself for finding a way out of this restrictive mess I was in. I realised that I could use the head of my department to my benefit in this situation as well. This man had been a completely ineffective manager, who needed to justify his position by assigning pointless tasks and publicly berating all the staff that was beneath him. He was intensely jealous of the relationships I had established with many of the pupils and teachers; where he on the other hand had not. The students recognised him for what he was and wouldn't warm to him.

A week before, I had handed in some reports, but he refused to accept them because he wasn't happy with the way I had structured one of the sentences. Even though I knew there was nothing grammatically wrong with this passage, and I double-checked it with the head of the English department who agreed with me, he insisted that I change the sentence before he would accept it. If I didn't, he threatened that this would cause my report to be delayed and that I would be written up for tardiness. I was certain he was acting out of his displeasure with the recent NQT issue, of which he had limited understanding. Because of this, I refused to change the sentence just for the sake of appeasing his unnecessary demand.

When he realised that I had not cowed to him, he came rushing down the corridor where I was talking with some of my year eleven pupils. He was yelling and flailing his arms at me, reprimanding me for being disobedient, as if I was a child. I was incensed at his audacity in such a public setting and I sunk to his level, shouting back until we were engaged in a full-force shouting haggle. I stood my ground, refusing to change the sentence that was grammatically correct just to meet his preference. I left school that day in a huff, and listened to the advice of a colleague in my department to take the next day off as a sick day so that the situation could calm down. Unfortunately, my absence just made the issue worse.

When I went back to work the following day, I was immediately called into the office of the assistant head of faculty and told that I had been labelled as disobedient staff and it would be nearly impossible to live that down. I was so disheartened by the unfairness that I wanted to take the day off too, but several other teachers happened to be out so I was told that there was no way they could forgive me if I left that day. I gave in and attended to my classes. As the afternoon approached, however, I was called into a meeting with one of the school's deputy heads, who explained to me that my absence the day before proved that I was a waste of the school's funds. I tried to stand up for myself and we entered into a debacle. She wasn't being fair and I felt too hurt and mistreated. I resigned on the spot, without even remembering I had just signed the paperwork for a mortgage on my first home in the UK.

As soon as I calmed down, I realised what a tremendous mistake I had made when I was in a snit. I shamed myself for once again not being able to handle conflict gracefully and mindfully. But, that's who I was, a young woman who ran from conflict rather than facing it head-on and fighting the battle to the end. The day was just around the corner when Jasmin and I would complete our sale agreement and move in to the house I had just gotten a mortgage for. Yet, now I had no idea how I was going to pay for it. My head raced with the fear of our situation. I wondered if there was any way I could call the mortgage company and cancel the sale, but everything was done, the papers were all signed and I was holding the key to unlock another burden in my life.

"Ego can ignite a satisfaction so deep within us, regardless of the consequences."

Chapter 14

"Money is a prison for those less fortunate to have been born without it."

The first month that my mortgage was due came quickly and there had been very little work where I could earn money. I was unaccustomed to the employment practices of the UK and I didn't realise that I could register with multiple agencies to increase my chances of finding employment. Gradually, I became savvier and the work began to trickle in. By the beginning of November, I had only worked a total of three weeks over the past two months. December wasn't any better, and I only managed to find work four days out of the entire month.

Our savings were rapidly dwindling down to nothing and I asked myself continually how I could have been as stupid and egotistical to put us in this situation. The proud part of me would always retort, "How dare they treat you that way?" Certainly, I had grown up poor, but I had some dignity and I was sure that they were cheating me at that school. But, in my anger and haste, I had robbed myself; no one forced me out – that was all my own doing.

The jobs I found through the other agencies were in the teaching profession. But, instead of getting a classroom of pupils that I would teach on a daily basis, I found myself running from school to school. One day I could be assigned to a school in East London, the next day I could be in the north, and the next in the southwest. I felt dizzy and unsettled at the constant moving about, but I couldn't complain because the bills were being paid. For the second time in my life in the UK, I lamented, I had given up stability for instability.

But, I was now immersed in the life of supply teaching and I just had to deal with it.

Of all the schools I was assigned to during this hectic period, the one that stuck with me most was a special needs school. This school catered to children who suffered from various disabilities, and the student population ranged from mild cases of Down's syndrome to severe cases of cerebral palsy. In my short time there, I met a young woman named Charlotte. She was a pupil in my classroom and even though she was eighteen years-old, she had the body of a twelve year-old and hadn't ever learned how to speak. She was mentally unable to participate in the lessons, and instead she would just want to sit next to the adult in the classroom and run her nose all over, smelling them and contemplating something unknown in her head.

I was so distraught by the experience of working in this school. The sight of the children in their wheelchairs or with assistants physically supporting them brought me to tears. I thanked God for the health of my child and realised that I was not one of those special people who had the internal strength to deal with these children on a daily basis. I tried my hardest to soften my heart and get over my own upset at seeing their situation, but I was unable to do it. I felt like a terrible person whenever a wave of nausea would hit me after seeing some type of regurgitation as an assistant was attempting to feed a child. Many of the children had to be fed through tubes.

I remember one child in particular who looked perfectly normal among the mass of other physically challenged students. I focused my attention on her to keep from crying in the lunchroom, and I wondered why she was here. One of the assistants set a chocolate cookie on the table in front of her, and while she showed interest in it, she never made an attempt to pick it up and eat it. When I asked one of the assistants what her ailment was, they explained to me that she had a severe stress anxiety disorder that inhibited her ability to carry out even the simplest of tasks, such as feeding herself.

The day didn't get any better after lunch time, and I had to rely heavily on the assistants, especially when there was a situation involving a child soiling themselves as I was not trained in medical hygiene care or the subtle social care that was needed to address this type of situation. I prayed that I wouldn't have to come back the next day, as I was completely unequipped both professionally and personally to deal with this type of student population.

The high school I was assigned to the next day was set in an immigrant area of the city and was largely composed of students that were from African nations. I learned the lesson that day that sharing a skin colour does not equate to sharing a culture. The children were louder than I had ever experienced. Every conversation was carried out at the top of one's voice. I kept trying to 'shush' them in the hopes of creating the Jamaican decorum. One of the permanent teachers watched my fruitless efforts for a while and then came over to explain to me that in many cultures in Africa talking softly in the presence of other people was considered extremely rude because it indicated that you were trying to secretly talk about the others around you; loudness was the African decorum.

There was one boy in my classroom that was surprisingly louder than all the others. When I tried to engage him in the lesson, he instead focused on my obvious West Indian's heritage and began making a slew of disparaging remarks about people from my region. I addressed this by explaining that I may be Jamaican by birth, but am African by origin. He was pleased with my remark, announcing to the class that it was a good thing to hear that I embraced my origin, but that some in the Caribbean don't.

I used the opportunity to explain to the class that this might be due to the fact that our fellow Africans had sold us into slavery and that's how we wound up in the Caribbean in the first place. Many people can't forget that to this day. I was shocked by his retort. He said that all of the Africans who were sold into slavery were the lowest and the weakest of their people; that they weren't good enough to be worthy of staying with the better part of their race. His prejudice attitude made me want to vomit – even more so than when I was faced with a mentally-impaired teenager the day before who had pooped himself and managed to smear the mess all over. My heart was sick too, because I knew this ignorant kid's views echoed what he heard at home. I wondered to myself, was there any hope for the future?

This experience was not my only introduction to prejudice that day. During a science lesson that I was sent to cover for a teacher who had fell ill, I was, at first, happy to find a Jamaican girl among the pupils. However, one of the boys in the classroom was very focused on bullying her. Right in front of me, he announced that all Jamaicans were born with a criminal record. I could not believe what was going on in this school! I felt like so many of these children had poisoned minds at such a young age.

This was definitely not the environment I wanted to be in everyday, my spirit couldn't stand to be constantly belittled like this. Little did I know that someday in the future I would marry an African man, have a child with him and look back on this experience for some clarity about our interactions.

Since my career as a supply teacher provided no permanent job, I became very frugal, saving for the ever-present possibility of there being no work on any given day. I was taking any job that was offered me, in fear of the same eventuality. On one day in October 2006, I didn't receive the usual early morning call for a placement. Instead, I used the morning to attend a parent-teacher's conference at my daughter's school. When I arrived, the teacher showed me a poem that Jasmin had written. The poem was entitled 'ANGER'. While the teacher focused on the exceptional cadence and advanced word usage, I focused on the message and realised that this hectic existence I was leading should not interfere with my time with my child.

I was not a neglectful mother by any stretch of the imagination. I never considered the time I spent with her a sacrifice of time that could otherwise be spent making income. I loved every minute we would spend in the evenings doing her homework or simply talking about her day over dinner.

"When all around you seems to be a whirlwind, just stand still and allow the calm to take effect around you. It will sort out the chaos".

CHAPTER 15

"Societies differ and can make or break you, so you must be mindful to stay unbroken as those same societies will eject you if you are weakened."

The home I had purchased was a flat located on the third floor above a street-level café. Upon first glance from the street, it looked like an eyesore, but once I stepped inside, it was as if I had stepped into a charming cottage straight out of some fairy tale, set in hushed forest. However, I soon found out that this serene calm only existed when the owner of the flat below was away from home. Turns out, the previous owner of my new flat had neglected to mention that his reason for selling was because of the nightmare neighbours that lived below.

My first encounter with this reality came the day after we had moved in. When I met these neighbours in the building's entrance, they were blatantly cold towards me. I thought they may be upset at the noise created by our moving in, but my apology was met with nothing more than a hostile dismissal from their presence. I soon found out from the neighbourhood gossip that these people hated all blacks and were very vocal about their dismay that 'niggers' were coming into their building.

I handled the situation by steering clear of them whenever I saw them, and making sure that our house was very quiet so they would not have anything to complain about. However, my attempts were all for nothing. These people wanted Jasmin and me out, and as soon as possible. I started receiving threatening and derogatory messages on my front door. When I ignored these, hoping that their interest in this campaign would fade if they got no response, they began a more aggressive campaign. Now, whenever I was in the buildings common areas, no matter what hour, day or night, the neighbours would suddenly appear, pulling their pet Rottweiler and leaving enough slack on the leash for him to run at us viscously and snap his jaws at us with only a centimetre or two to spare. They would even leave the dog in the stairwell, the only exit for my flat on the upper floor, so that Jasmin and I would be trapped in our home.

The situation only escalated from there, and turned into an outright campaign of harassment and threatened violence against myself and my young daughter. When the situation got too dangerously close to physical violence, or when I would fear for our lives, I would call the police, if nothing more than to document the threats in case we were found dead in our apartment the next day. Unfortunately, this whole situation fell under the definition of a civil matter, and until the people caused bodily injury to us, there was nothing concrete that could be done by the authorities.

I reverted back to my all-consuming, stressful environment. The threat of the neighbour's hatred and their snarling dog was as bad as the threat of the four gunmen I had fled from in Jamaica. I was also under massive stress at this time to continue to afford the mortgage payments. Since my work was not stable enough, I found a flatmate to move in with us and ease this financial stress. The lady who answered my advert was kinder than I could have ever hoped for. Abina quickly became my confidant and dearest friend, filling a place in my heart like a sister. Together, we bore out the trials with the downstairs neighbours.

Despite the fact that the troublesome neighbours would raise hell if even the smallest of noises crept out of our flat, they would routinely host all-night parties, often going on full-force until the sun started to lighten the morning sky. We would simply try to sleep through it all, but some nights were just too much and both Abina and I had work the next day. On those nights, one of us would steel our nerves and go down to politely ask to have the blaring music turned down, explaining the late hour and our need for sleep. All we ever got in return was verbal assaults or threats that they were going to get the dog on us. Invariably, we would find used needles and alcohol bottles in the stairwell the next morning. The stench of marijuana would permeate our walls and cling to everything in our upstairs flat. I worried constantly about Jasmin being exposed to the drug smoke that clouded the stairwell and wafted in through our adjoining ventilation system.

The couple that occupied the downstairs flat fought with anyone who they encountered, including their party guests and each other. The fights between the couple were epic! She was always drunk and he was always high. During their most violent blow-ups, which always happened outside of their apartment door, I would have to intercede to help protect the young woman from the beating her partner was giving her. Yet, her gratefulness never extended beyond the few minutes after she had been saved from his pummelling fists.

I never saw either one of these people keeping a routine work schedule. We soon figured out that neither held a job, but lived off of government subsidies for the disaffected. However, most of the social help they received was immediately translated into alcohol or drugs. The rest of their money went towards the latest technology and luxurious items I could only dream about having. It was shocking to see the material items these two could acquire while never holding down a job.

Meanwhile, Abina and I were working our butts off and struggling to make ends meet. By summer, I was really in financial trouble. Not only was I in arrears for the TV and the telephone bill, but I also had a large amount of debt on a credit card, for which I couldn't afford anything beyond the minimum payment. But things soon got worse when the bank holding my mortgage sent a certified letter stating their intent to take me to court over a complicated matter involving paid bills that were misclassified in their system and accruing massive late fees and penalties.

Now, I had to hire a lawyer to help me rectify the issue, which was growing more serious every day. Anyone who has dealt with a lawyer knows that not only do they cost significant money but they also require a significant amount of time to help them adequately understand the situation they are addressing. My free time and every extra cent I had, started going to the lawyer fees.

Things were getting so bad that one morning I had to spend the majority of the single pound I had in my purse just for postage to send some required documentation to my lawyer. When Tobore dropped Jasmin off shortly thereafter, I panicked with the thought of how I would be able to afford food for her. She would be hungry, the refrigerator was empty and I only had twenty pence in my wallet.

The phone rang and I was greeted with a less than lucrative offer from one of the employment agencies I was registered with. The consultant asked me if I was available for work. When I said yes, she became very chipper. On the other hand, I became more despondent as she talked to me; the work paid little and out of that, she told me, I would have to pay her two hundred pounds out of each week's wages. On the face of it, the amount is paltry, but when you are living pound to pound it adds up. I kept thinking how a full five days fee would be two hundred pounds, which equated to one 'costs' too many or a portion of the week's groceries for us. I wound up taking the job. People in my situation have no other choice but to accept the terms that in the end benefit others.

These experiences with temporary employment served to remind me of the importance of higher education. I recognised that having a solid education and firm set of degrees behind your name were critical steps towards steady employment and a more secure life. I stressed these ideas to Jasmin, and supported her in every educational pursuit. She excelled at her studies naturally, but I was always there to push her further so that her life would be easier than mine was.

The next job placement I was offered was in Luton, which is about an hour away from our home by train. I struggled with the idea of the long commute and how much of my time it would take away from all of the other things that needed my attention, but an old Jamaican adage kept creeping into my head: "When a man is drowning, even a moving mosquito is an option". However, my apprehension melted away when I heard that the job was permanent.

Before the lady from the agency provided any of the details of what the work would be, I accepted. I knew that whatever the tasks were I would work my hardest to master them. All that mattered to me at that moment was that I was finally gainfully employed. I let out a joyous shout of praise to God.

"Struggles can be medicinal."

CHAPTER 16

"While trying to carve out your own destiny, you sometimes leave dents in someone else's."

The new job afforded me a stability that I had not had since I first arrived in London. I was catching up on my bills and adjusting to the long commute. Things were finally starting to come together for me and I was so relieved, but the calm was only a temporary break in the storm of my life.

Shortly after starting my new job, I received a frantic call from my family back in Jamaica. The news was that my sister Anna had been picked up by the police and was currently sitting in a jail cell. At first I didn't understand what I was being told. How could my thirteen-year-old sister be in jail?

I was told that after I left for London she had run away from home. I immediately felt a twinge of guilt. You see, I was the one who had made her move back into my mother's home before I left Jamaica. She had come to live with me right before I left, but she had cultivated a clandestine and inappropriate relationship for her age with a much older boy who was my helper's relative. My only way to curb the situation, and hopefully stop her from getting pregnant or taken advantage of anymore, was to send her back home.

Apparently, she was terribly unhappy back under my mother's thumb and she absconded in the night only a few days after I had left for London. I was shocked that no one had bothered to share this news with me until now. The excuse was that none of the family knew where she was. They had reported her disappearance to the police, but even the police didn't seem very concerned about it. The general consensus was that she was just being a rebellious teenager.

However, now that she was locked up in jail, everyone realised the seriousness of the matter. When my mum called to talk about it, I could tell from the tone of her voice that the situation was much worse than I had imagined from that first phone call. She said that the situation my sister was involved in was so scandalous that it was even being covered on the nightly teToboresed national newscast.

I didn't need to hear another word. My family back home needed me and I felt partially responsible for putting her on whatever path it was that led her to this sad state. I used every last bit of credit I had to purchase a plane ticket back to Jamaica so that I could meet with the local bank and try to secure funds for her bail. I called in to take some days off of my new job, dropped Jasmin off with my sister, and went on a mission of saving Anna from the treacherous situation she had gotten herself into.

When I arrived in Jamaica, I was given a rude awakening to an unforeseen consequence of my having left the country. I had taken the title for my house in Jamaica to use as collateral for a loan to make the bail, but when I started to fill out the required forms I was informed that any money I had would be ineligible for posting bail due to my resident status in another country. There was nothing I could do for her.

With this bad news, I went to visit my sister in the juvenile centre where she was being held. The sight that greeted me broke my heart. Here she was, separated from me by thick black metal bars. Her eyes were wide with fear. I ached with the desire to save her, to tell her that I was there to take her away. When I told her that the law forbade me from helping her, she began to weep uncontrollably. The pain in my chest was tangible, like someone had scooped out my heart and left only a raw, gaping hole.

When I left, I went immediately to my mum's. The information came flowing forth from every family member that came by. They had found out that my sister had been living with some unsavoury people who had a very bad reputation around the town. Apparently, she had become intimately involved with a man who was on Jamaica's national most-wanted list of criminals. The news only got worse from there. People had told them that she was known to carry a gun, and flash wads of cash around. I couldn't stop picturing the little girl I knew (play acting) as a character living in the wild, wild, West.

But this was nothing like a child's game of Cowboys and Indians. As I sat listening to this almost unfathomable information, I began to take stock of my surroundings. My mum's place, while still humble, seemed much nicer than it had been when I was last there. The longer I was there, the more I noticed subtle changes in their entire lifestyle. If this had been twenty years ago, I would have thought they were rolling in the dough, so to speak. From what I could tell, though, nothing else had changed.

However, the matter at hand involving Anna completely overshadowed my curiosity about this. The conversations shared that evening, with different family members, ended in the same way; everyone lamented how embarrassing this was for our family as a whole. She had brought a great shame upon us, which flowed throughout the entire community. I was told that people were now openly accusing all of us of having supported and benefited from her unsavoury exploits.

I finally got the full story about the situation she was involved in that led to her arrest. She had accompanied a group of boys when they went to rob a supermarket. Things got out of hand when the owners resisted and the boys ended up killing them. They had almost gotten away with it, but the group was living in a rented home and when they stopped paying the rent, the landlord sought to eject them from the property by reporting to the police that they had a stockpile of guns on the premises. When the police searched the house they found a multitude of guns and ammunition, some of which matched the evidence from the supermarket killings.

I couldn't believe what I was hearing. I felt like I must have fallen into some Hollywood thriller movie plot. How could this be real? How could my very own sister, who was still a child, be involved in this sordid affair? Robbery? Murder? I couldn't make the information align with reality. In the end, I had to catch my plane back to London. There was nothing I could do for Anna and my job and child were waiting for me back in our UK home.

My life in London continued on as if the horrible plight playing out in Jamaica did not exist. Finally, I received word that Anna had been released and was living once more with my mum. She was on probation and needed to report to the police every day. My mum told me that she was very calm and quiet, staying at home and not even trying to go out. We both expressed our relief that she must have learned her lesson and had been scared straight out of her dangerous lifestyle.

It quickly became apparent though, that Anna wasn't merely acting out a penance to her wild ways. She was simply staying indoors and sleeping a lot because she had a general sense of feeling unwell. We all equated her malaise to depression and didn't give it much thought beyond that. As the day of her trial approached, however, the family noticed an alarming deterioration in her physical appearance. Again, we all thought it was the stress of the trial that was taking its toll on her overall health, and when she was found innocent of the serious charges of accessory to murder, we were sure she would perk up.

We were completely mistaken, however. Over the next few days after her trial finished, her health deteriorated at an alarming rate. One of my sisters called me in a panic, asking me to come home right away because they didn't know what to do, but knew that something was terribly wrong. They had gone to visit several doctors, but none could come up with a diagnosis.

I had just surrendered my passport to the home office for my visa to get extended. I therefore couldn't make any trips outside of the country. I felt trapped and helpless. The news that came from home was worse every day. Finally, God performed a miracle and my passport, along with Jasmin's and Tobore's, arrived at my house by post. I immediately went to the travel agent and bought plane tickets for myself and Jasmin.

I spent the next day's packing and getting our London lives in order during the time we would be gone. The day before we were to leave, I was exhausted and fell into a deep sleep mid-afternoon. My nap was interrupted by the jangling of the telephone and the weight of Abina coming to sit beside me on the bed. Her hand on my shoulder was so gentle, as she leaned in to whisper to me to wake up. Before I put the telephone receiver to my ear, I knew something was dreadfully wrong. It was my sister's voice on the other end, telling me that Anna had just died.

I couldn't believe what I was hearing. How could this be? She had just been to a new doctor and they had again found nothing wrong with her. She was scheduled for an exploratory surgery that morning. We all knew that she would have a diagnosis soon and be starting the treatments for whatever was causing her illness.

I crumpled to the floor as the truth of what I was hearing sunk in. Even after my sister had hung up, I sat frozen onto the wooden floor in my flat, unable to move or even hang up the phone. The disconnected buzzer alerted Abina to come and take the phone from my hand, but I never heard it.

When I was able to move again I knew I had to change our tickets to fly out that night. Unfortunately, I could not simply change the flights. Instead I had to relinquish the old ones, apply for a refund, and purchase new ones. Since the refund would take up to eight weeks to be processed, I was stuck without the necessary funds to afford two flights. The only way I could afford to go home now was if I went by myself, leaving Jasmin, but accompanied by Kem.

I travelled to Jamaica on my own, and met with my family to bury our little sister. The funeral was a low-budget affair, and most of the cost was left to me since I was still the most successful of our family. It was also up to me to identify her body in the morgue and claim it for burial. While I picked through her clothing to choose something for her to spend eternity dressed in, I thought the sadness would kill me. I was also left to deliver the eulogy at the funeral service and I was at a loss for words that could adequately describe the absolute tragedy of her last year of life and the unfairness that she would not be allowed to live it out and redeem herself in the community's eyes.

My poor mother was in so much distress; I began to fear for her life as well. Although I had grown up seeing her suffer the life of the desperately poor, it was nothing compared to the suffering she was experiencing now. The grief radiated from her, permeating the entire family. I was again plagued with guilt for leaving my family to pursue a new life far away. I couldn't stop wondering if Anna would still be alive had I only chosen a different life path.

After the funeral, we received word from one of the doctors she had seen in the days leading up to her death that they had finally come up with a diagnosis; lupus. I also found out that she had been baptised in the church right before she died. She was merely 19 years old. Gone too soon.

"Death is a thief, it robs us of our loved ones and keeps a hold of all the person is and was."

CHAPTER 17

"Some events in life can rob you of your soul, but our bodies function nonetheless."

The death of my little sister changed my life in more ways than I could have imagined. I became fiercely protective of my own child. I felt like I could leave nothing to chance when it came to her future wellbeing. I swore to myself that she would never find herself feeling unloved or unwanted, as a kind of guarantee against her feeling the need to seek out security and intimacy in friends or lovers who could turn around and take advantage of her.

After we laid Anna to rest, the journey back to London was a hard one for me. Not only was I drowning in my sadness over this lost life, but I was weighted down by the knowledge that I had spent my very last penny. For the first week of my return, I could think of nothing but memories of her. My heart ached with the unfairness of the situation; I cried out to God, asking why the young had to be taken before the old?

Anna and I shared a birthday and I kept playing back the memories of all the celebrations we had shared together on that day each year. The memories were sweet, but caused as much pain as they did comfort. Both Anna and I had been born on the 28th of February, but when my birth was registered the officials made a mistake and wrote 22nd February on my birth certificate. This had never caused any problem, so the family just ignored it. But since my sister's death, I could not find joy in celebrating in her absence and I accepted the 22nd as the day that was for me alone, burying all the happiness of the past along with my sister.

The Luton job had fallen through due to my travel back to Jamaica, so I was back at square one, waiting for the phone to ring each morning with news of any temporary position. The positions were very few and far between, so I registered with as many employment agencies as possible, not caring what the industry was that they served. I was ready to take any work, as long as it brought in money.

The first job offer I received was as a contracted cleaning lady for a large firm. Since there was nothing else coming my way, I swallowed my pride and forced myself to go in with a bright spirit. The whole way in, I chided myself for thinking this job was beneath me. After all, I took Jasmin's and my rubbish out to the bin and dust our house every week, how different can it be? Well, the answer to that question came the minute I met my new supervisor. Apparently the job wasn't so much general cleaning, but was specifically scrubbing public toilets for ten hours.

When the supervisor told me about the job's sole duty, she gave me a swift look up and down, and commented that I wasn't dressed for the job. I must say I was happy to hear this, thinking that she would find another duty for me to earn the day's pay, but it was not to be. She dismissed me, despite my assurances that I was willing to do whatever they needed of me.

As I left the building, my eyes were already stinging with trying to hold back the flood of tears. I felt like I had reached my lowest point. I couldn't even get a job as a toilet cleaner! By the time I reached the bus stop, the tears were running freely down my face. I couldn't get on the bus while I was blubbering like this, so I ducked under the bus shelter to get out of the rain and called my friend Jade for moral support. She comforted me and we prayed that God would see me through this rough time and lead me down the right path that would provide work for me and an income for my family.

In the next weeks, work opportunities continued to be scanty, so I began looking for alternative means for helping to afford the basics of life, such as food and utilities. When I looked into the possibility of getting help from social services, however, I found that my immigration status inhibited me from receiving government-funded assistance. As I look back on those times, I cannot imagine how we survived, but we did. It was only by some miracle that there was always food in the refrigerator and light that came on when we flipped the switch. We must have had an angel following us around all of those days.

During this time, I worked *very* hard to conceal my emotional distraught from my daughter. I wanted to spare her the burden of worry and continual anxiety over financial matters. She was only a child and needed to be focused on her studies and her friends. When I sunk so deeply into depression that I was having difficulty functioning in daily life, I took anti-depressants to help lift me out of the blackness that was clouding my entire outlook on life. But the doctor's visits and the medication added more strain on our nearly non-existent budget.

When I reached the end of my wits and there was nothing left in my control, I lifted my voice in prayer, crying out to God to help us out of this hole I had dug us into in London. The next day, I got a call from the agency that had originally offered me the teaching job in far-away Luton, which I had lost when the situation with Anna occurred. I couldn't believe my luck when the agency representative told me that the position was open again and it was still for employment on a permanent basis. There was no hesitation on my part this time. I took the job immediately and praised God for His mercy.

The distance I would be commuting back and forth each day necessitated child care for Jasmin for the hours she would be out of school and I would be travelling on the train. God was again merciful in this situation and I found a Jamaican lady named Afua, who had lived in the UK for some time, but had outstayed her visa so she couldn't obtain employment otherwise. Unfortunately, the arrangement didn't work out for long.

After the first two weeks, she seemed to have lost enthusiasm for the job and started showing up later and later each day. Abina had a job that was closer to our home, so on those days she could stay longer than me, waiting for the lady to show up and take charge of Jasmin who needed escorting to her school. Finally, the morning came when Afua never showed up. I was on the train, on my way to Luton, when Abina called to tell me that Afua had called to say she wasn't coming in at all that day.

I didn't know what to do, and I was in a panic. I was half-way to Luton already and there was no way I could get back home to Jasmin before Abina needed to be at work. Abina could hear the distress in my voice, and she told me that she would call in late for work and escort Jasmin to school. I was so grateful, she was an angel sent by God. But, I was still left with the problem of finding reliable care for Jasmin during my workdays.

Unfortunately, the challenge proved insurmountable and I had to resign from my position in Luton shortly thereafter. Meanwhile, the contentious relationship with my downstairs neighbours was still going on full force and escalating by the day. The week after I had given up my permanent position in Luton, I had one of my most frightening encounters with them. I had decorated the stairwell on my landing as an extended area of our home. Besides the several plants I had cultivated to give a fresh feel to the atmosphere, I had placed a picture of my dream car, a Ferrari, on the wall to serve as a motivator for me to keep up with the struggle of making a success out of my endeavours in this place. I had also put up a bright light, so that we could see up the stairs when we came in at night.

The landing was a private area, and was accessible only by a locked door, for which only Abina and I had the keys. When I arrived home late one night after running some errands, I found that there was no light in the stairwell leading up to my flat. It was pitch dark and I became very afraid, thinking of the neighbour's vicious dog. Maybe he was resting in the stairwell and would attack if I surprised him in the dark? I started up the stairs on tiptoe and was flooded with relief when I neared the landing without incident. However, I started to notice something coarse crunching beneath my feet.

I reached the door and fumbled to get my key in the lock in the darkness. When the door opened, I was able to see by the light on the landing that I was treading on smashed remains of the bulb. The sight on the landing itself was even more sinister, though. The Ferrari picture had been obviously moved, the window that opened into my home was smashed, and all of my plants and pots were gone.

I was certain it was the neighbours, and I could not handle the harassment any longer. I thought of sinking to their level and calling on some friends of mine who lived in the roughest area of Brixton, imagining these tough guys coming around to scare them into behaving. But, this was a silly wish, and I knew I had to overcome the challenge that these people represented.

I was now back to full-time job hunting and accepting any temporary position that came my way from the various agencies. The jobs I took ranged from call centre representative to ironing clothing and babysitting.

I knew one way out of this mess was to get more education for myself, so I took any savings I could scrape up and enrolled in courses at a local college. The coursework was exciting, and I loved having something to stimulate my mind again. In fact, some of my fondest memories were made when Jasmin and I would spend our evenings together doing homework at the small dining room table in our little flat. I was determined to make our lives better and I instilled the importance of education in my daughter so that she would never find herself in such a fix.

"Being a mother shouldn't just apply to your biological child, but should transcend to each child you come into contact with."

CHAPTER 18

"Someone else's errors can be the penalty of the innocent."

I had been terribly distraught about having to quit my job because of my child's day care needs, and I was very angry with Afua for being so unreliable. In my head, I was blaming her for my dissatisfaction with my life, but I soon made a complete turn-around and started sending up prayers of thanks for her poor work ethic. This saved me from a disastrous situation that was brewing at the school where I used to work in Luton and which I had been completely unaware of.

I found out through the temporary staffing grapevine that the principal of the school was into all sorts of trouble and was let go, along with most of the newly employed teachers (of which I would have been one), only a few weeks after my start date. This mass exodus gained everyone involved a bad reputation for being part of whatever shenanigans the administration was up to, even if they were on the periphery or not involved at all.

I realised that Afua's acting up was really a blessing in disguise. God was looking after me, after all. All of my efforts to re-enter a teaching career could have been destroyed and we would have been in an even worse position. Moreover, I had even been considering moving Jasmin and I to Luton, only to have wasted all the expense and effort and be left with no job. I had already put our flat on the market, and that at least remained a good decision because regardless of my job situation we would be out from under the burden of the mortgage.

I made a quick trip back to Jamaica to sort out some bits and pieces regarding our citizenship and residency status. I needed to apply for new birth certificate, since there was some new movement in the Jamaican government system that necessitated re-issuance of old birth certificates. I took my old white one and went down to Spanish Town, where the official office was. I had met a man from this area over the internet many years before, and we had kept up a genial online friendship – nothing romantic – for all of that time.

His name was Alfie, and our online communications were sufficient enough for me to feel comfortable staying at his place(as through our communication I soon discovered that my family knew him very well and he had a good relationship with my mum), even though we had never before met in person. I was still under the impression that Jamaica remained the trustworthy place that I had grown up in; I was blissfully unaware of the ways its society had become depleted morally. Luckily, God was again watching over me and I was safe in Alfie's house.

On the second morning of my arrival, I woke early and left for the registrar's of births and deaths office. My plan was to be first in line so that I could get my new birth certificate and spend the rest of my time visiting family. Man, was I in for a big surprise! I was called forward by one of the first workers to open a window for service, and was greeted by a lovely lady who looked over my plain white paper certificate and directed me to enter the inner offices. I was so proud of my posh new British accent and the immaculate way I was dressed, thinking how it really was paying off in a professional setting and earning me better treatment.

I was taken into a secluded office and to my surprise, met by the same women but this time with a very stern look on her face. She informed me that I was in very serious trouble for having tried to pass off a false document. I was totally confused, what did she mean by false document? I explained that I had had this birth certificate from the time I was a teenager, when my parents applied for an update regarding my father's name being listed on the certificate. She asked exactly where I had gotten the document I was trying to pass off. I told her that my parents had given it to me. She gave a slight smirk of disbelief, and I realised that there was a serious problem at hand.

I had never questioned the authenticity of this document. I had even used it to secure my visa to enter the UK and never had any trouble. The lady informed me in a very official tone that I was in possession of a false birth certificate and whipped out a large book filled with others that looked exactly like mine. She flipped from page to page, pointing at the signature line on each, and told me that the signature was falsified. I was in total shock. I again explained that my parents had obtained the certificate and given it to me when I was still a minor. I then asked how it could be such an obvious forgery as she was suggesting, since I had used it to get my passport, my travel certificates, my degrees, everything in my life that required an official governance approval.

Instead of answering, she told me she had to call in the police; this was an offence that necessitated a criminal charge. I couldn't believe what I was hearing, the police? Was this woman mad? I had just come down to get a new copy of my birth certificate, and now I was being threatened with handcuffs and a criminal charge. It was as if I had entered a nightmare. I flashed back to the terrible juvenile detention facility where my sister was held, and I knew that the Jamaican jails for adults were much, much worse. A wave of panic rose up in me.

The lady told me to stay calm; she had already called the authorities. I was locked in the little room until they arrived, and those minutes were tortuous and I fretted over this confusing situation and how I had come to be in the midst of it. Surely, I thought, this was all a mistake or I would simply wake up safely in my bed and breathe a sigh of relief that it was all just a bad dream.

Finally, a group of men in uniforms came filing into the room. They stated in official barking tones that they were a special force from the fraud squad and were here to collect me on the charge of fraud. I couldn't even move to stand up from my seat. This was my first time being in such proximity to lawmen that were looking at me as a target. They firmly gripped my upper arms and helped me to my feet, escorting me directly out of the building and into the police car waiting outside. I was driven down to the fraud squad office, which was located in downtown Kingston.

I didn't utter a word for the entire drive, even though they kept throwing questions at me about how I had managed to get into the UK with this false document. All I could think about was being jailed and stuck in Jamaica awaiting a trial, unable to get back to my daughter, who would be thinking her mother had abandoned her and not understanding what was happening. I figured out that I was actually getting more brusque treatment than anyone else because of my British status.

I was taken into an office and a guard was placed outside, while I waited for whatever my fate was to be. It was nearing noontime now, and I was hungry. The guard on duty checked in and said he would send someone to fetch some food for me. Finally, I was visited by the interrogators. They asked all of the same questions that had been fired at me during the morning hours, and repeated all of the same charges they were levying against me. I could only reiterate that I had nothing to do with this, that I was telling the truth about how I had come in possession of the document that had never before been questioned by any other governing body. But, they weren't interested.

I was allowed one phone call, and I called my mum to ask her to come down to the station to help explain the situation – better yet, I said, please have my dad come, after all he was much closer since he still lived in Kingston. My mum said that she would come, but it would take some time as she would be traveling from St. Elizabeth. She also said that there was no way my dad would be coming. Apparently he was too afraid to enter the police station and become entangled in this mess.

I found out later that my dad said he didn't feel any need to be involved because he had only agreed to make his status official on my birth certificate by changing my last name to his own because I had wanted it for so long as a child. If I had known back then what the price of this small token of ownership would be, I would have opted to keep my mum's maiden name and would have happily maintained my outsider status.

My mum made the three-hour journey by bus and when she arrived, she helped the police to coerce my dad to come in as well. I remember those phone calls vividly, with the officers assuring him they weren't going to arrest him because I was the one in custody. They finally convinced him to come in when they told him all he needed to do was give a statement so that they could determine what to do with me. My mum cursing him to within an inch of his life also helped. I almost fell over with relief when he finally made the twenty-minute trip to the station from his house and I realised that I may be released so that I could be allowed to go back to London to be with my daughter.

My mum and dad were interviewed in separate rooms, to see if they would corroborate my story. I was petrified about what might be going on. Would they provide any new information? Would I be hauled off to jail? I was not in the room when my father finally gave his official statement, and the truth came out. He admitted that when he went to change my name on the birth certificate, he didn't go into the registrar's office. Instead, he gave my original certificate to one of his brothers who lived nearby and who knew someone that could get a 'bandulu' one for much less hassle and much less money. The bottom-line was that he had produced a fraudulent document that I had been carrying around and showing off to all governmental agencies since then.

The whole ordeal of my parent's interrogation took only about one hour, but it felt like an eternity to me. When the officers came back to the office where I was being held, they produced the written statements that my parents had given and told me to sign off on them. I was shaking with relief and my signature was a wobbly mess. The officer who took the papers from me said that I was one very lucky lady to have the opportunity to get out of there.

I wasn't sure what he meant, but it became clear when he explained that I now had to pay one hundred thousand JA to get free. This was all done under the table as they say in Jamaica. I was furious! But I kept my outward calm, knowing that no misbehaviour would be tolerated in this situation, no matter how justified. I hadn't done anything wrong, but here I had to pay for a crime that my dad committed and admitted to. As I gave up the money for my freedom, I steamed inside, thinking that if my dad had only claimed me from the time of my birth, this would never have happened.

I was finally allowed to leave the police station a free woman, but my day with the authorities was not over. I had to go back to the registrar's office, along with my dad, in order to get the situation completely cleared up. He was required to sign some official forms so that the name change could be officially approved. I was still fuming from the unfairness of it all and demanded to see the head of the office, who came out and was delighted to hear that I had gotten it all cleared up. My joy did not equal hers, though, and I demanded to know why I was punished for something that could have been just as easily proven by a phone call from their offices? And, I wanted to know why I was the one arrested when the people who made my certificate, without my knowledge, were the wrongdoers? She listened to my rant and apologised, explaining that the office had to follow protocol, but also saying that there were many others out there just like me who were innocent participants in others' crimes. She even said that she was thinking of how the office could provide amnesty for these cases.

I was granted an expedited new birth certificate, and when I got it in my hands, I couldn't wait to hop on the next plane out of Jamaica. I returned safely to London and held my baby tight and told her how much I love her. As I explained the situation that had nearly kept me away from her forever, I was reminded of how quickly our ordered lives can spiral out of control. A deep-seated dislike towards my father blossomed that day, and I gained a greater respect for my mum.

I arrived home to an offer on the flat and praised God for his mercy. I had even managed to make a small profit on the sale which provided some security while I tried to figure out our next move. I was still convinced that purchasing a home was better than renting, so I looked for a house that was more in our budget and found one in Mitcham. While I waited for the sale to be approved, Jasmin and I had to move in with Tobore and his flat mates. We wound up staying for about six weeks, and the experience of Tobore and I living under the same roof again was strange, but not unpleasant.

The house they were in at the time had ample space and Jasmin and I had our own room. In a way, it felt like our life towards the end of Tobore and I's relationship with us residing in separate rooms, but getting along cordially in the common areas. I suppose our being back in this familial-type living situation stirred something in Jasmin's mind, and she began to recall our life in Jamaica, when we lived in our dream home and before that fateful night of the attack. She even began asking questions about what had happened to make us leave, which led to more pointed questions about strange men with guns and her other flashes of memory about that night. I could not muster the courage within myself to revisit this painful memory, but I didn't know what else to do. If I had been in a more stable situation myself, I would have sought out intervention from a professional who deals with traumatic events, but I didn't.

We finally obtained the house and were able to move in. I was so relieved to have a safe place, away from drug addled neighbours and their vicious dog. In this home we even had our own front door, with no communal space. Our new neighbours turned out to be absolutely lovely, and we settled in nicely. We even had a lovely garden space, where Jasmin could play and I could find some peace while tilling the soil by hand and planting flowers. I didn't mind that this place had a tiny bathroom and rather flimsy tub, the freedom I felt here was invaluable. I felt like my life was finally progressing, like I had begun to grow roots in this country and had found somewhere that I would no longer feel like a stranger.

I realised that having a house of my own was something that gave me a sense of security, like nothing else did. Maybe it was because I grew up with my mum not having one for herself, or maybe it was the constant moving around that I did as a child. I always felt unsettled, but when I had a house, I also felt like I was safe on my own, like I didn't need a man to provide for me.

My professional life was going steadily, and I had work daily. However, there was a strong governmental push at the time for teachers to have their Qualified Teachers Status, known in short as QTS. I sought to get the QTS certification, but I was lacking math as a subject for my education degrees. In Jamaica, accounting was considered a math subject in college, and during my time in high school, our main math teacher was suffering from diabetes and was constantly on sick leave, so I graduated without this subject. I did get some math lessons, but they were few and far between. In addition, I wasn't the brightest student in the class, so I always presented a challenge to the teacher, who chose to focus on the smarter students in her attempt to get her lessons caught up for the times she was off. The whole situation made me hate math.

Now I faced another problem. I couldn't get the QTS because of my missing math credits. I also didn't want to own up to anyone that I was so severely lacking in this subject. Yet, I was still expected to teach it. Sometimes, when I had to cover for a math lesson, I would sit and stare at the text books, terrified that the students would start asking me for detailed explanations. I couldn't tell a logarithm from an exponential, and the thought of having to discuss algebra frightened the life out of me.

I was so far behind in my math skills that no amount of study would catch me up in time to achieve the necessary QTS. I conceded defeat and started looking for a way out of the teaching profession. I thought of the irony in the end of my teaching career. Originally it was me who didn't like the field and thought it was beneath me, but in the end I was not good enough to stay in it. That's not to say I was a bad teacher. I was actually very good in all the other subjects, and I genuinely cared for my students.

When the reality finally hit that I was no longer allowed to teach, I grieved as if I had lost something as important as my husband or my sister. It hurt just as much to be rejected by a system as it had to be rejected by a loved one. I had given so much of my life to this career, and I experienced a real heartbreak when it was taken away from me. Here I was, in London, a single mother with a new house, having to close another chapter of my life; what could possibly lie ahead?

"Heartbreaks are not always caused by people or intimate love gone wrong; they can come in unexpected forms, and I have had my fair share of all types."

CHAPTER 19

"Sometimes, just swimming into the waves is all you can do, letting the tide carry you to the destined place."

It was coming up to Easter 2007, and I was at my wits end trying to find a job through the agency. My opportunities for teaching had dwindled to nothing without my achieving the QTS, but more worrisome was the fact that summer was nearly upon us and the pool of job seekers would soon be flooded with my fellow teachers who were unemployed between terms. I was back to taking any job offered so that I could ensure enough money came in to pay the mortgage.

I realised that this high-stress and unstable lifestyle was not sustainable over the long-term. So I began to work towards completing my master's degree in business administration. My daily life was so full of my activities to chase a paycheque that I had no social life to speak of. The thought of seeking out and finding a life partner hadn't even crossed my mind. Besides, if I were to be honest, I'd have to admit that I still considered Tobore to be the missing partner that completed our little family, and in some ways, I didn't feel like I was missing anything.

I still was dealing with the persistent issues of having to keep my schedule flexible enough to be available for my child and be ready for any situation that may arise with childcare. Every parent deals with these issues, but it is no secret that they are even more of a burden when you are assigned as a temporary staff, where the administration is much less forgiving when hiccups arise in the daily schedule. I began to feel like I was giving my own child the same instability that had marred my childhood, and this is the one thing I had promised myself I would never do.

I threw myself into the work of finding a stable, permanent job. Soon, I had applied for so many jobs that I couldn't even remember what I had applied for. When people called, I was completely confused about whether the job was temporary or permanent, what the job itself was, and how I should present myself to make the best impression. I was a mess, and finally I felt the burden of it all crush my spirit. I had managed to buy a little car in the previous year – there was no getting round it anymore, with the available jobs being so much more widely scattered than feasible by the bus routes.

One afternoon, I got into the car and drove to some nearby woods where I hiked out into the field and sat down on the grass and cried. In my grief, I turned my face to the heavens and asked God to answer all of the blasphemous questions that had been hanging at the back of my mind for so long now. Why was He punishing me? What had I done wrong that had attracted His wrath? Why did He give everyone else a smooth path in life, while He made me fight for every step along mine? Why did He stand by and allow me to be knocked back five steps for every one step I took forward?

No answers came booming down from the skies. I felt so alone and broken. I couldn't let my precious child see the utter distress I was feeling, so I pulled myself together and put on a calm and cheerful face to greet her at the end of her school day. I even took her on a quick jaunt to the park, so that she could play, and for at least a while, feel the carefree spirit that I had never experienced.

In a way, being outside of the house was also an escape for me. For a short while, I could clear my mind, of the dreaded letters that were coming with bills I had no idea how I would pay. When we returned home that day, the pile of letters was waiting, just as I had feared. I took a deep breath and sorted through them. It was one after another with big red writing, signalling an overdue account and calling for immediate action. But one envelope in particular caught my eye. It looked like regular, non-threatening, business mail. I selected this one to open and discarded the others in a heap on the table.

As I began to open it, I remembered all of the job applications I had put in and started to remind myself that this was probably just a run-of-the-mill rejection letter. To my surprise, it was a letter from a well-known supermarket chain inviting me to interview for their on-the-job graduate management programme! I didn't recognise the location where the programme was going to be held; some place called Erith that was southwest of London. That was no matter to me, I didn't care how far it was as I would drive there everyday if need be.

It looked like God was looking out for me after all. In my excitement, I went and purchased a cheap, but nice, power suit. On the day of the interview, I arrived at the site to find a slew of other applicants, all anxious and dressed professionally. We were a diverse group, each of us representing a different nationality and age. They put us all in a waiting room and we sat in awkward silence for a few moments. It seemed that no one was willing to break the ice, so I took it upon myself to ease the tension in the room by starting to engage each person in a group conversation. Soon, we were getting a sense of where each of us hailed from and our current situations.

It was here that I met a young man, near my age, named Tre. He was of German and Cameroonian descent, and I was instantly attracted to him. His demeanour was so classy, and he had an amazing sense of style. His dark suit was cut perfectly to fit his extremely tall and sinewy body frame, and the colour complimented his dark skin. I was smitten. We were called in for the interviews in turn, and the process was gruesome. At the end, though, I found out that I was among those selected to return to attend the second round of interviewing. I overheard Tre getting the same news, and my heart leapt when I realised I would get the chance to see him again.

I kept our chatty conversations going from there, and by the end of the second interview, we exchanged numbers. I was given the promise of a dinner date as well. But I did not get any news that day of an invite for the third interview session. I thought maybe they weren't letting people know directly this time and went home with a light heart from my flirting with Tre.

When Tre and I met for dinner, however, I found out that he had received word shortly after the second interview about his being invited back for the third round. I went home and rummaged through all of the mail for a second and third time, hoping to find an envelope that I must have overlooked before, but there was nothing. My heart sank. I really thought I had done a good job in the second interview and this was the most promising career lead I had had in a long time.

The next day, I resigned myself to the fact that I was going to be rejected from the programme and I got myself ready to visit yet another employment agency to see what jobs might be coming up. As I was stepping out the door, my phone rang. It was the supermarket administration, and they were inviting me back for the third round of interviews. I was thrilled and determined to knock their socks off when they spoke to me next. This interview was to be held the next day at one of their stores that happened to be located very near to where I lived. I sent up a silent prayer of thanks to God. I couldn't believe that I may land a job that was within a stone's throw of my home, that I may be able to stop this crazy commuting schedule that had me travelling all over London, from pillow to post.

The interview was even more intensive than the first two; I felt like I was on trial. This was the business world I was re-entering, and it was so different from the teaching system that I had been immersed in since my arrival. The interview consisted of cognitive skill tests as well as physical skill tests. I was given pallets to pull and pack; this was hard and heavy work. I couldn't imagine that this type of manual labour would be part of the role they were expecting me to fill, especially after all the administrative type interviewing of the first two rounds. They had me count items on the shelves, work the cash register, and help with the end-of-day accounting and deposit of money into the safe. Basically, I had a go at every duty that any employee would perform in the store on a daily basis.

One of the hardest parts for me, however, was seeing all of the cash being counted at the end of the day; I was so envious. Here, I was, only rarely making ends meet while working my butt off and I couldn't imagine having this kind of income. It was a torturous test for my psyche, and I battled to not fall prey to my downtrodden emotions.

When the interview ended, I was sent home with no idea of where I stood or when they might contact me next. The pessimistic side of me thought that they hadn't given me an answer straightaway because I must have failed in one of the important tasks; maybe I hadn't packed enough on the shelves or maybe I hadn't been fast enough on the tills? I began to lament that I was again back at square one. My nerves were frayed and I went directly to my friend's house and cried my eyes out with her. She comforted me and reminded me of God's unfailing love, which I was still doubting. She left me alone to think, and I wrote this prayer to the Lord:

Dear God, why have you given up on me? What sins have I committed that are so unforgivable? Why, regardless of how hard I try, does nothing seem to work out for me? Why don't you just take me in your protective arms and prevent me from going through all of this pain, suffering and shame in front of my friends, my foes, and my child? Was running away from Jamaica not enough punishment? Was being held at gunpoint not a hard enough experience to endure? What more shall I be required to go through, to give up, in order to be worthy in your eyes? God, please release my blessings. I am in need of a miracle, right at this point in my life. My mortgage is due, and after I pay it, Jasmin and I will have no money left. My bank account is empty, the bills are piling up, and I have this beautiful and innocent child that I have to shelter and feed. Lord, remember that my family, especially my mum, still depends on me. Lord, please help me.

I left the prayer at my friend's house and went to my home to face my mounting debts and the sadness that was threatening to take me over completely. I made dinner for Jasmin, tucked her into bed, and laid myself down to sleep. A week passed and I heard nothing from the supermarket, so I started reaching out to people around town for stints doing cleaning work. After two weeks of this, I couldn't take it anymore. The dust and cleaning solutions would cause such severe allergies that I would have asthma attacks. But, there was nothing else for it; I had to make money somehow.

As I finished my most recent cleaning job in Shirley, I decided to treat myself to a pint of lager. Jasmin was staying with a friend and I had the evening to myself. I pulled my car up and parked at a nearby pub garden that my friend said she would meet me at.

Right then, my mobile phone began to ring. The ringing of a phone had long since lost its appeal for me, as it was almost always a debt collector on the other end of the line. I was certainly in no mood to fend one of them off.

As the ringing continued, I began to worry that it was family back home calling, but that too turned me away from answering. More often than not, a call from Jamaica was only made to ask for money, any contribution I could make to cover school fees, medical expenses, or clothing. The requests seemed never-ending, especially since they thought I was living a rich life across the pond, no matter what I told them to the contrary. I thought of how my cupboards at home were empty, how the money I had made that week from cleaning was barely enough to buy groceries that would last for only a few days and how the car petrol was low. I reached over and switched the phone off and headed inside to forget for just a moment that my life was not so pathetic.

The alcohol did just the trick. It took away all my pain and eased the nagging worries that plagued my mind. I rarely ever drank, so I became quite tipsy rather quickly. When it was time to drive home, I didn't even care that I was still feeling so light-headed. As a matter of fact, a part of me wished that the journey home would end with me just being taken away by the angels, spirited away to a place where there was no hunger, no embarrassment, and no weight of responsibility on my shoulders. This life I lead in London, hand to mouth, was slowly killing me.

When I finally reached home and parked the car in my driveway, I decided I was still numb enough from the alcohol to hear whatever stressful or bad news was left on my voicemail. I was shocked to hear a voice identifying itself as a caller from the supermarket chain who was letting me know that I had successfully passed the final interview and offering me the management job at the very store I had tested at on the last day. I was struck dumb; I couldn't believe the news I was hearing. I didn't even realise that tears were streaming down my face, unbidden. I must have sat in that car for more than thirty minutes, just crying and staring out into the darkness. Ultimately, I was able to move. I dropped forward onto my knees in that small space in front of the driver's seat and I sent up a heartfelt prayer of thanksgiving and worship.

When I gathered myself together, I made my way inside and had a dinner of baked beans and eggs on toast and I saved a portion for Jasmin, in case she was hungry when she got home. I called the friend who Jasmin was visiting, to tell her that I was on my way to pick up my daughter. She instantly noticed the uplifted tone of my voice, but assumed it was due to my having found a man. No, I chuckled at her; there was no Mr. Right that was causing my euphoric state. I had found a permanent job which was much better. Before I started driving, I made a call to Tre, to see if he too had gotten the job offer. He hadn't and my reward turned bittersweet.

The salary they offered was great, especially considering the pittance I had been working for, and the thought that it would arrive on a consistent schedule was almost too hard to believe. It had been over four years since I had made a monthly salary. The job was to start with a one-week training session that was scheduled at a location rather far away from my home. I was going to have to find someone to look after Jasmin. I began to panic, thinking that childcare issues might again foil my chances of attaining stability in the workforce.

I finally decided to reach out to my sister, Kem, and ask her to stay with me again. Considering our difficult times in the past, she wasn't my first choice, but I couldn't think of anyone else. In the time since we had lived together in that filthy little flat back when she had first arrived, she had birthed a daughter. Coming to stay with us now included her child, and I knew this ultimately represented a greater financial burden for me. Even though Kem was currently unemployed and spent her days watching her own child, she insisted that I pay her for her time taking care of Jasmin and include the cost of food for both of them, plus free board in the house. She knew I was in a bind and not in any position to deny her demands.

With Kem and her daughter settled in to watch over Jasmin, I left for the week of training. I began to feel a little bit comfortable about my situation. For all the distrust I had for Kem regarding our relationship, I did not fear that she would fail to take care of my child. I thought this situation may even work out in the longer term, with her being home for Jasmin while I worked at the store near my home. Unfortunately, I discovered rather quickly that I didn't like the job at all. Yet, there wasn't much I could do it. I needed this job desperately, and I would just have to suck it up.

The people who visited the store and the people who worked under my supervision were so rude, and there was nothing to be done about it. Every interaction had to end with me putting my tail between my legs and letting the other person feel like they had bested me. The job also included all of the physical duties that we ran though in that on-site interview. Apparently, there was nothing a store manager didn't have to do, from picking up trash in the trash car park, to cleaning up any mess in the aisles. My workday didn't end after the store closed either. In the after-hours, I was expected to fully wash the floors and lift heavy boxes for stocking. I realised my managerial job was really nothing more than a glorified cleaner/stocker.

I did have the responsibility of tallying up the sales at the end of the day and depositing the money in the safe, but I also had to work the registers and ring people up throughout the day. Rather soon after starting this job, I was transferred to another store that was a bit further away, and told that this store was to be my 'mother store'. This meant it was the store where I was to stay for the duration of my tenure with this company. The hours remained long, and I found myself going to work before Jasmin had awoken in the mornings and coming home after she had gone to bed. I was hardly seeing her at all, and this was taking a toll on me. Kem told me that she was also pining for me, and that she wasn't happy.

Over the next few months, I continued to date Tre, but for some reason, things never turned serious with him. I found out that the reason was his womanising ways. He had nine children with six different mothers. On top of that, he was legally married to one of them. He tried to explain to me that his wife was back in Germany and he needed women to comfort him in her absence. He told me he had women here, there, and everywhere and that I could be one of them. That offer did not appeal to me. He was far too carefree for my liking.

We managed to remain friends, even though deep down I was mad that he hadn't been the man I was hoping he was. Being in his company always made me feel special because when we would walk down the road, girls would lap him up. It gave me a nice inner feeling that I was the one he had chosen to be with that night, and I would laugh privately in the knowledge that if they knew all of his secrets like I did, they would probably turn him away too. The proverbial last straw in our relationship was broken one night when he made the crucial error of leaving his mobile phone at my place. One of his many women called and when I answered it, she warned me off her man! Oh dear, if only she knew that she didn't need to. I quickly assured her that I had no interest in taking him and I counselled her to think the same.

The job was taking a toll on me physically and emotionally. I found out that the other managers in this job had been there for years, yet they were still classified as deputy managers. It was blamed on company politics, and I was advised that the only way up was to keep your head down and your mouth shut. Kissing ass never hurt either. The way to help ensure a pay raise or promotion was to put in even more hours without any complaint. Asking for vacation time or sick leave would drop you back to the bottom of the pool. I felt trapped. To me, the more work you put in, the more they took advantage of you.

I realised rather quickly, too, that I had significantly more real-work experience in the business world than the majority of the managers. This fact did not gain me any friends among the management staff, though, and I was viewed by many as a threat. I found out that all of the other managers, except the manager who was supervising my programme, were former cashiers. They weren't happy that I came in and started at the top, while they had to work their asses off to get there.

This hostility manifested in our workplace. When new processes were introduced, or I found an old one that I was unclear on, I could never count on help from my colleagues who had an intimate understanding of the supermarket's inner workings due to their long history with the company. I whipped out my sales personality, hoping to charm my way into getting people to come to my aid. This only ever worked with the cashiers, and never with the managers. In many ways, the experience of working with these people was like being back in grade school. They would sabotage one another, making the tills short at the end of the day or offering to help and then leaving things half done. Really, they would do anything they could to make each other look bad.

The challenges in this job extended beyond the management and cashier staff, and went up to the executive level. The regulations that guided our workdays were proof of this. There was an unwritten rule that no one was to leave the premises during their lunch hour. Even the cashiers would quietly grumble that this was time they needed to go pay bills, make a doctor's visit, or deal with issues involving their children. It was apparent to all, however, that this practice kept the whole staff available for dealing with urgent matters as they arose, regardless of the fact that these urgent matters were always the result of chronic understaffing.

At one point, I was even instructed in how to keep cashiers on shift who were trying to leave, regardless of them having completed their workday hours or the urgent need involving children that was calling them away. No cashier could leave their post until they were tallied up and cashed out by their manager. In my role as manager, I was told to simply ignore a cashier's bell, which signalled their need for my services, and busy myself with any mundane activity so that the cashier would have to stay on for as long as possible. Leaving one's post before being cashed out was grounds for immediate sacking; the cashiers had no choice but to stay until I made my way over to tend to them. The thought of doing this to someone else, especially another parent whose child was waiting at home hungry or to be picked up from childcare or school, put my stomach in knots. I couldn't bring myself to do it, and I wondered at the way other managers could even ignore young mothers standing at their registers and crying softly because they were torn between the needs of their awaiting children and the need to hold onto their job.

Herein was where a worker would place his or her self in a further bind by following the rules. One of our star workers, a young man named Elton who was a single father, was a perfect example of this. Like all parents, he had childcare issues. But, instead of being honoured for his stringent work ethic, he was routinely exploited for the good of the company. If he reported a potential upcoming conflict in his schedule, such as a parent-teacher conference that was scheduled before his shift that day that may make him slightly late, Elton's schedule would be restructured to completely obliterate that time off so that he would have to show up earlier than scheduled, miss his child's conference, and ensure that he would not miss one minute of work.

My refusal to play the corporate games earned me the mocking title of 'softie manager' and scored me no points with my bosses. There was a rumour floating around that the company had already blackballed me from any types of promotion. I found myself once again stuck in a dead end job and lacking momentum in my new career field. Was this to be my fate forever?

"The unknown is wrapped in cycles of belief and dare-to."

CHAPTER 20

"Reputations can attach themselves to us and become a permanent part of our person."

Things remained difficult at the supermarket, but I maintained my gratefulness for the job and the opportunities it promised for a long-term career in administration. But, the longer I was there, and the more I became aware of the inner workings (or lack thereof). I became disillusioned with the managers who were supposed to be mentoring us as trainees. Things really started to disintegrate for me over a three-week period, when I struggled with making a simple request to be allowed time off of work to meet in-person with my bank to rearrange my mortgage. I followed the company's policy for making such a request, yet each time I asked my direct supervisor, Sam, our store manager, for an hour off during a single day of work, I received the clipped response of "Not today."

The deadline set by my bank for completing the necessary paperwork was rapidly approaching. I was getting very anxious about how to resolve this conundrum and finally decided to take one of the days in lieu owed to me, instead of pestering my supervisor anymore. Asking for lieu time presented its own challenges, particularly because this time was routinely denied under some vague explanation that involved the inaccurate scheme in which we were never allowed to report overtime hours worked.

I knew that my daily overtime, like everyone else's, had not gone unnoticed by my colleagues and my manager, and I prayed that Sam would be fair when considering my request. I began to prepare for approaching him. I first carefully checked the corporate schedule and that of my local store to find a date when my absence would be least disruptive. The upcoming Friday looked perfect. Moreover, I decided to not simply take the day off, but instead to request to exchange my rota with that of another trainee manager, Emmanuel. That way, the other staff would not have to cover the duties of an absent trainee manager's.

I showed up on Monday prepared to present my idea to Sam, but found that he had taken a day in lieu. I was not surprised to find that he had not made any attempt to cover himself, and I felt good about myself for having such respect for my colleagues as to avoid the uproarious situation that this always led to. As the day wore on, the staff came upon a few small situations in which we needed the advice of Sam, I volunteered to make the call – thinking that I could be clever and use the call to also discuss my rota exchange idea with Sam. However, as soon as I brought up the rota exchange, Sam cut me off with a simple response of "There's never much to be done in the store, so don't worry about it." My heart sank when he hung up the line. I knew this statement didn't reflect the truth of our working conditions; there were tons to do, and the staff and I were living proof that very moment as we were all scrambling to take over Sam's responsibilities in his absence. I knew I could never act so irresponsibly towards my co-workers.

On Tuesday, I again showed up ready to present my reasoned ideas for rota exchange to Sam, but again I found out that he had just called in to take yet another day in lieu. I checked Emmanuel's schedule and found out that he wasn't scheduled to be in again until the next day, so I would have to finalise my whole plan with both Sam and Emmanuel first thing tomorrow morning. When I reported for work that Wednesday, the first person I met was Sam. We exchanged our

Ava Brown

normal friendly hellos at the canteen door and made our way inside to get ready for the day.

I had planned to lock my purse up in my employee locker and pop into Sam's office for a quick chat before either of us got overwhelmed with the daily routine. But, as soon as we walked into the welfare area, a stocker named Kumar came up to us and started telling me that the employees from welfare had just been discussing the on-going problems with everyone getting their requests for days in lieu approved. I felt a flicker of excitement, thinking to myself what perfect timing this was since Sam was still standing right next to me. Kumar went on to explain to another employee, Michelle, had suggested that a good way for the staff to get the lieu time owed to them was to accurately record all the hours we worked in a single day. She had even gone as far as to question the legality of the current practice the company had of inaccurate recording.

I could sense Sam's growing agitation. He had stayed silent so far, but now was the time for him to stop this blasphemous talk once and for all. "We cannot do that. The District Manager will go ballistic about it." I was surprised at his strong tone of voice and tried to lighten the situation by telling Sam that I found it hard to believe that the company's administration would not want to at least hear the suggestion of something that would ensure we were within the boundaries of the law. Sam simply shrugged and said that such topics of discussion were not for the day's start. He turned on his heel and beckoned me to follow.

As we walked, I figured there was nothing for it but for me to put my request to him at that time. I was relieved and a bit shocked when he merely sighed and gave verbal approval for my time in lieu that Friday as well as for my exchange of rota with Emmanuel. We even chitchatted a bit after that, before I headed to the warehouse to start my workday in earnest.

A little over one hour passed before I finished my tasks. As I began to make my way to the main store, I was delighted to see Emmanuel and I waved to catch his attention. Before I could speak, though, he started yelling angrily at me, saying that someone had just told him that I had changed my shift with him without asking. I rushed to clarify the misunderstanding, telling him that I had only gotten permission to ask him if we could exchange shifts and that I had been waiting for him to come into work that day so that I could talk to him about it.

Emmanuel said that Sam had just told him that the exchange was already complete. He was understandably angry with me, thinking that I had disrupted his schedule without any forewarning or consideration for his opinion on the matter. I couldn't get a word in edgewise and before I knew it, he was pointing a finger at me and saying that since I had taken it upon myself to mess with his life that I would have to come in on Friday night after closing to pick up the store keys for opening on Saturday. I was a bit blustered at this point, and stammered that I couldn't come in that late on Friday night because my child would already be in bed, and besides, I wasn't scheduled to open the store on Saturday morning; Sam was. I asked, couldn't he just give Sam the keys when their shift together ended on Friday night? But, Emmanuel just glared at me and stormed off.

I went to see Sam straight away to get this messy situation resolved, but he was busy with the cleaning contractor and unavailable for a discussion right then. Emmanuel was refusing to even look at me and I realised that the situation, though unintentional, had been unfair on him. I needed to resolve it and take care of myself without involving him. I peeked back into Sam's office, but he was still with the contractor. He knew what I was seeking him out for, and when he saw me he simply pointed to the stack of rota sheets for me to take and fill out. I changed Emmanuel's shift back to its original schedule and marked Friday as a lieu day for myself.

Not too long later, Sam came storming out of his office, waving the rota sheets in the air and yelling at me to "Come with me right now!" I was shocked at his red-faced anger, and said, "One moment, please, let me wrap this up." He barked out, "I said come with me right now. This is more important than what you are doing." He was bearing down on me, and I had a flash of the men who had attacked me that night, waving their guns and coming at me with a similar cold look in their eyes.

My first instinct was to cower, but within seconds I found my voice to stand up for myself. I steadied my tone and said, "Please calm down and please don't talk to me like that. We shouldn't yell at each other in the workplace." This set him off. He shot forward and screamed in my face, "For fuck's sake! Come with me now!" I steeled myself and stayed standing upright, staring directly into his eyes I told him that I wasn't going anywhere with him until he calmed down and apologised for cursing at me.

He must have been dumbstruck by my unexpected refusal to cow to him because he stood motionless with his mouth hanging open. I took advantage of the moment and reminded him I had never been rude or disrespectful towards him and that I didn't appreciate his rudeness or his undermining approach. Not surprisingly, the ruckus had attracted the attention of all the nearby staff, who started edging away. Sam began to realise that all eyes were now on him. He took a deep breath and stepped back from me, quietly saying a quick "Sorry".

That's it? I thought. This whispered utterance was absolutely unacceptable as an apology. Before I knew it, I was telling him that he knew my name and that he needed to apologise to me properly. He set his lips in a hard line and gestured for me to follow him into the welfare area, where we would have some more privacy. Instead of getting the apology I was expecting, however, he turned on me and said firmly that it was his privilege as my manager to speak to me however he saw fit, and asked how I dare embarrass him in front of his other staff.

It was fortuitous that he had led us to the spot right in front of one of the corkboards with random company news, announcements and policies tacked onto them. I immediately noticed one of the company's policy sheets and grabbed it down off the board, pointing to the paragraph that specifically addressed this exact situation. I reminded him that this way of addressing me was considered harassment. He went back into his silent mode and stared hard at me. As the moment of silence stretched on, I turned on my heel, gathered my belongings, and left the store.

As soon as I arrived at my home, I called our District Manager, who was Sam's direct boss. He wasn't in, so I left a message telling him that I needed to speak with him urgently regarding an inappropriate and explosive situation at the store. He called back shortly and I was able to tell him what had just transpired. He agreed that Sam was out of bounds, and that an employee should not be spoken to like that under any circumstances. He told me that he would start working on the situation.

About an hour later, the District Manager rang back and asked if I felt I could work with Sam again. I replied that I could work with this man again, thinking that time heals all wounds and sometime in the future we would likely cross paths as our careers were parallel in this company. To my surprise, though, the District Manger responded by telling me that he needed me to go back to working under Sam within the hour. I nearly started crying when I explained to him that I didn't feel comfortable going back into the situation so quickly after what had just happened. My breathing calmed down when he said that he understood my apprehension and asked if I felt that I could finish out that day's shift in another store instead.

When I agreed to this alternative plan, he said he would arrange something in the next hour. In the meantime, though, he wanted me to just drop by my home store and have a quick chat with Sam. "It will be good for the relations of the store", he explained. I reiterated that I didn't feel comfortable talking to Sam right away, and I said that I was happy to go, just on another day. I was shaken to my core, though, by his response. He said, "OK, Ava, you have left me with no choice but to start a formal investigation."

For the second time that day, I found myself stammering out an explanation to defend myself against an unfair attack. Sam had been so angry and so disrespectful. Having to interact with me right now because his boss was ordering it was unlikely to ease his upset. I didn't make any headway though, and the District Manager told me he would have to figure out what to do from here that fit within company policy.

When he hung up, I rang my home store straight away. Sam answered, and as soon as I identified myself to him, he said that he was actually angry with me for four things that day, but I had not let him talk to me about them before I had chosen to leave the store in a huff. I had not expected this, and I could not imagine what these four things could be. After all, the day was still young and I hadn't even been at work that long before our situation exploded, and he hadn't seemed bothered by anything during our first morning chitchat session.

He began to tick them off, one by one. First, I was in the wrong for calling him to ask work-related questions on his days off. Second, I had been in the wrong when I had left a message for Emmanuel about wanting to talk on Wednesday when he came in (apparently, Emmanuel said my tone was abrasive). Third, I was in the wrong about an ordering mix-up, which actually had nothing to do with me and I knew for a fact was his own screw up. And, finally, that I was in the wrong for modifying the rota on the scheduling sheets that he had pointed me to.

I immediately tried to defend myself, reminding Sam that he had told me to call him at home with work-related questions. This was a common practice among all the staff, as sometimes important items couldn't be found when he was gone and he needed him to tell us where to locate them in his absence. My temper began to boil at the unfairness of it all. I justified my role in the situation involving Emmanuel, explaining that my intent was to protect my co-workers by having someone cover me when I was out so as not to be a burden.

I asked if he had listened to the message I left on Emmanuel's phone, and if he agreed with the assessment that I was rude? He said he didn't need to listen to anything, he already had the word of my co-worker and that was all the information he needed. He then brought up the conversation in which I told Emmanuel I would not be able to pick up the keys on Friday night. When I started to speak, though, Sam cut me off and said that it didn't matter what my excuse was, I needed to make allowance for doing anything that anyone told me to, even another trainee manager. He ended the conversation by telling me not to waste my breath on explaining any of my actions or defending myself, he had already made a judgment on me and the case was closed.

I could not believe that in the end, I was the one who was going to be put at fault for this entire situation. I felt utterly used and disrespected. There was nothing more for me to do but wait to hear back from the District Manager and learn my fate. When the call finally came, I was surprised to find out that I wasn't the one being transferred and it was Sam who had been reassigned to another store. There was a new manager by the name of Adelaide and I was to report to her the next day.

When I showed up and introduced myself, it was evident that Adelaide had been briefed about me. The way she looked at me made me feel like there was a sign above my head that read 'troublemaker'. The stress of the situation the day before still had me on edge. My asthma was acting up but I felt there was no way that I could take a sick day, with the previous day's events still so fresh in everyone's minds. I spent the morning wheezing and gasping for air as I pulled around the pallets of newly delivered vegetables and completed the stocking of the shelves. Adelaide noticed my struggles and inquired in a tight voice if I was ok. I told her that I wasn't feeling very well but she just gave a short response of "hmm", rolled her eyes, and went on with her business.

The other workers were more solicitous in their concerns for me, coming over to help me with the unpacking. One colleague even went to Adelaide and told her that my audible struggles to breathe were making him scared for my life, and he thought maybe I should go home early. This only earned him a loud rebuke, in which she snapped at him and told him to stop being an "interfering git." She then called me over and told me in a low voice that she was on to me, she knew all about the tactics that staff would come up with to get out of putting in a good day's work and she wasn't about to put up with any of it.

By this time, my breathing had become so ragged and I was getting so little oxygen that I passed out. I could hear someone calling for an ambulance and feel myself being carried out to the car park into the fresh air. The ambulance turned up in no time and whisked me away to a nearby hospital. I found out later that as soon as the ambulance was called, Adelaide had started rushing around to act as though she had been concerned and that she told as many staff as would listen that she had only leaned in to tell me to go home for the rest of the day but that I had turned her down and insisted on staying to work.

In the meantime, the hospital staff gave me a nebuliser which immediately eased the constriction in my lungs. I was physically and emotionally exhausted by the time I was discharged to go home, with strict instructions for bed rest. The doctor had told me stress was the most likely trigger of this severe attack; he gave me a written advisement to take a three-day break from work. In my off time over the next few days, I wrote a letter to the Regional Director, outlining what had really happened over the past week and that morning with Adelaide. My hope was to somehow correct the injustice of the whole affair and regain my esteemed standing with the company.

Since I had witnesses who could attest to the truth in the matter, my complaint garnered a formal acknowledgment that Adelaide's behaviour had been inappropriate. I was disappointed that there was to be no consequence for Adelaide's actions, but when I returned, I found a new policy pinned to the corkboard that said any employee who was in physical distress should be dismissed to go home or to a doctor's office immediately. At least I was assured that the company hoped to avoid this situation happening again to any other employee.

I also found out when I returned to work that I was being immediately transferred to another store. The new store was further away from my home, but I felt like my reputation was tainted at this one and I was relieved for the chance to start afresh. I quickly came to realise that the spots on my professional persona extended company-wide, though. After one week at the new store, I still had not been entrusted with the duties involving cashing out or taking the cashiers' money to the safe. This is one of the key responsibilities of any mid or senior level manager, but my duties were kept to no more than those of a cashier. When I wasn't at the till, I was put on C-checking duty which is where an entry level employee would walk up and down the chillers and check each stocked item to ensure that the sale-by date hadn't passed. It was this duty that made my demotion the most obvious.

Still, I didn't make any complaints and did everything I was told. My tactic for restoring my reputation was to be the perfect yes-man. However, after a month of this strategy, nothing had changed. I finally mustered up the courage to ask my manager if the job title I had been transferred under was different from that I had at the last store, but he said that I was still a trainee manager. I wasn't sure how to respond to this, so I left the conversation and waited until I got home that evening to place a call to that manager to ask him about the details of my upcoming schedule in compliance with my trainee managerial status. He was very congenial and said that I was set to start taking over cashing-out financial duties soon. He told me that anytime someone was transferred, it was company policy that they learn that store's tills and the stocking-related duties before they moved on to the administrative stuff. I had worked with plenty of transfer employees before, though, and knew that this wasn't the truth. I was a special case.

"Exit strategies can creep upon us so unknowingly."

Ava Brown

CHAPTER 21

"Removing one brick from a stack can send walls crumbling down. Quickly escaping isn't always possible so we sometimes get crushed."

At long last I was given the cashing out and closing up responsibilities befitting of my trainee manager status. I breathed a sigh of relief and thought for sure I had finally redeemed myself in the eyes of the upper management. That day I was so proud when the money from the day's sales balanced with the money in the safe and I held my head high as I prepped to lock up the store. I gathered my personal items together and went to reach for the store keys that I had expected to find in my pocket, only to realise with a thrill of panic that I had not retrieved them from the manager's office before he had left earlier that evening. I ran to the office, hoping against all odds that he had somehow forgotten to lock his office door and I could sneak in and retrieve them without anyone being the wiser to my mistake, but there was no such luck that night.

I stood and pulled at the locked door for a full minute, even though I knew the door was locked tight. "Why? Why? Why?" I screamed in my head. My conscience taunted me with the answer, "You messed up! You are no good! They should have never trusted you!" I turned and fell back into the door, banging with my fist in frustration. "Damn!" I yelled out loud. The only way out of this mess would be to call the district manager, who had never forgiven me for my refusing to speak to Sam that afternoon of our frightening confrontation. Now, I was going to prove him right for thinking I was a waste of the company's resources.

I tried to steel myself for the phone call to him, and his last words to me echoed in my head, "This

Company isn't for the weak hearted. We speak bluntly and we expect our employees to accept their lot without complaint." I knew this time I would be in for a particularly awful berating, and I just didn't think I had the fortitude to handle it. I started to cry, but fought back the tears of self-pity. I paced the room and took deep calming breaths. Finally, the panic and utter dismay started to dissipate and I remembered that another manager had mentioned being in possession of an extra set of store keys due to a mix-up earlier in the week. I nearly collapsed with relief, and felt the full weight of my anxiety lifted when she answered her phone and agreed to come down right away and bring me the keys.

I went home that night with a cry to God for his mercy, but also with a plea in my heart for this tenuous situation I found myself in to somehow be resolved. I knew that I could not survive under this type of stressful working environment for the rest of my life, especially when my efforts were leading nowhere and I was killing myself to merely get back in the good graces of the big wigs.

That night after I put Jasmin to bed and settled myself in, I took the time to reflect on my situation and to try and figure a plan to get out of it. Writing in my diary always helped me to organise my thoughts and gain clarity on anything troublesome that I was facing, and this night, I was in need of such clarity.

April 2008
Dear diary,

Life here in London has been the most challenging I have experienced since my time at teachers' college back in 1993-1996.

At this particular moment, a number of factors are challenging me: finances (I owe over seven thousand pounds on credit cards!), my job (I hate it!), and the way I am belittled and pushed around on a daily basis (I am the most qualified person in that stupid store, but I am treated like the biggest underdog!). Why is that Lord?

I am disgusted by the people I work with. They are vipers, hypocrites and ass-lickers. I am surrounded by the lowest of the low.

I am in the middle of doing a re-mortgage on my house, and that alone makes me have to hang in there and just take all of the crap that I am subjected to every day. I have no other source of income, so either I put up with everything that is sucking the life out of my soul and pay the bills or I fight to save myself and I lose my livelihood. Then, the bank will reclaim the house and I will lose everything that I sacrificed for in this fucking country.

If it was me alone, I may even consider giving up right now, but I have to keep a roof over Jasmin's head. God, and now my sister and my niece are living here too. Her help is invaluable, but the extra mouths to feed and board have exhausted all of my resources.

So, really, I have no choice but to go back to work, even though ever morning starts with a panic attack and ends with another sleepless night as I toss and turn with the anxiety of what is to come as soon as I enter that damn store's doors. If I do fall asleep, my dreams are all nightmares about what will happen if my alarm somehow fails and I oversleep the 6am opening time. Certainly, I would be fired. I know I am at my breaking point because I have started reliving my attack experience every time the alarm goes off, my mind tricking me into thinking it is the shot of a gun aimed right at my head.

I know that I am not eating well; the stress has just killed my appetite. No one needs to tell me that I am just going through the motions at work. I hate the lifting, the cleaning of the floor, and the packing of the shelves. My hands are so calloused that I am afraid to shake anybody's hand when I meet them.

My life has reached a stage where every time I compare it with what I left back in Jamaica, I cry. I really want to go back home, but Jasmin doesn't. She is ever so close to her dad and it would kill me to leave her here in London while I went back to Jamaica. I see no way for me to be able to go home. I just have to hang in there and put my desires beneath hers. I wish that there was some way both of us could be happy, but it's not possible at the moment. This is the harsh reality of motherhood: sometimes you have to sacrifice your own happiness for that of your child. Maybe my time to be happy will come when she grows up? Right now, though, she is all I have and it would kill me to lose her.

To make matters worse her uncle is moving here, so she has one less tie back to Jamaica and she will now like to go back even less for the holidays, which are the times I look forward to like a drowning man looks for a lifeline. As far as Jasmin is concerned, London is home.

I hate so many things about being in this dreary country. The cost of survival is far too high. I have to take every hour of work offered, even late at night, even when my daughter is home sick. It kills me to come home at 1am and find her homework left open on the kitchen table with a note to me asking for some clarification of something she doesn't understand, and knowing all I can do is write her a note back before I have to leave at 5am. This is what our interactions have deteriorated to, notes written in the wee hours of the morning.

Tonight was an early night for me. I got home and in bed right before it turned midnight. I don't know if its exhaustion or my realizing the pathetic state of my life that is making me cry right now. My prayers asking God why my life has turned out like this have only been met with a stone-cold silence.

I am sick of struggling! I want to be able to enter the grocery store and buy meat without having to sacrifice other items on my list. I want to not feel like an outsider anymore. I want to go home. Or find a way out of this constant cycle of working to near death and breathing a great sigh of relief every time a bill is paid. Please God, hear my cry! Please help me!

I went to bed and hoped God had heard my cries that night.

When I went to work the next day, I found that new rota had been posted. The last day for me having the safe responsibilities would be the day before inventory day, yet I was now scheduled to have the day off. I asked the manager about this discrepancy, but instead of switching my day-off for another day, he asked me to come in on that day even though I was not scheduled to be in the office. I had become so downtrodden that I simply agreed and went about my regular work duties.

That whole day my heart bothered me. I needed a day off this week, as I had promised to take Jasmin out for the Easter holidays. I could not break another promise to her, as so far in this job, I was constantly making up broken promises to her. I went back to see the manager and asked him if we could please find a way to reorganise the schedule so that I wouldn't have to work an extra day this week. He told me not to worry, and assured me I would get a day off as requested, but it would be the day after the inventory was completed. It was the best I was going to get, so I rescheduled everything with Jasmin and finished the week without a complaint.

The night after the inventory was completed. I received a call from the district manager who asked if I could come in for a one-on-one meeting the following day. I explained that my rota had been changed to provide for the day off that I had to miss to accommodate the inventory schedule. I also told him that I had rescheduled all the arrangements with my daughter to fit with the store's needs, and now those were set for the following day. I still remember the sneer in his voice when he said to me, "And, you were very crafty in setting those plans to ensure that you have that day off. Well, it's not going to work." He told me I had better get busy changing my personal schedule around because it was not a request, but an order that I meet with the Senior Manager of Operations that next morning. He ended the call by telling me not to worry too much, the meeting would be brief.

Something in his voice put me on guard. An uneasy feeling grew inside of me. I began to wonder, had I done something terribly wrong at work that day? I wracked my brains for every movement I had made that day, every word I had spoken, but nothing stood out. Maybe he had found out about the key incident? I began to feel a sick feeling churning in my stomach and I realised I was afraid of this man. I was shaking so badly that I feared I would be ineffective in the meeting the next day. I called on my friend Shoa and asked her to accompany me to the meeting for moral support; she immediately agreed.

When Jasmin awoke the next morning, I explained that we would have to move some things around and get a later start to our fun day than we had planned. She was disappointed once again, and I could see in her eyes that she didn't trust me to come through with my promise to spend the day with her. I promised her that as soon as this one meeting was done, we would have the whole day together. When Shoa and I were walking out the door though, I received a call telling me that the Senior Manager of Operations was running late and the meeting had been rescheduled for a few hours later in the day. It was just going to be too little time to leave the house to do anything and just enough time to make me have to break the promise I had just made to Jasmin.

When Shoa and I arrived at the office, the receptionist took one look at us and told me that I didn't need to bring any legal representation into the meeting. I explained that this was just my friend, and the lady directed Shoa to a seat in the waiting area, and me into an inner office. As soon as I sat down in front of the District Manager and the Senior Manager of Operations, they handed me a letter and instructed me to go over its contents.

Even before I began to read, my heart sank. I was fired.

The two men were stiff and formal with me, simply dismissing me from the room. There were no false attempts at easing the pain of my being sacked. No one said to me, 'good job' or 'you tried, but the fit just wasn't right'. I emerged in to the waiting area in a daze and mumbled something to Shoa about being sacked. She immediately took over for where my spirit had shut down. She asked the two men who were hovering nearby what was the reason for this. To both of our surprise, they answered her directly, but only said that because I hadn't worked there a full year yet, they were not obligated to provide any explanation. I felt the world unravel around me. The last glimpse I had of the District Manager as Shoa took me gently by the arm to lead me out to the car park was of him slightly smirking. It was if he was saying to me, 'well, you got your day off'.

Over the next few days, I began to realise the extent of planning that had gone into this sacking. Apparently, my sacking came as no surprise to everyone else; they knew it was coming on that very day. I was the only one who was blindsided. I began to wonder, how stupid could I really be? How did I not see what was going on around me? However, I still could not get any concrete answers as to why I had been sacked. The most I got was one of the cashiers suggesting that it was almost my one-year anniversary with the company, when sacking gets a lot trickier from a legal standpoint and that in managements opinion, I was going to be the manager that went against the fabric of what they stood for, too nice to staff, my consideration and Christianity were stumbling blocks, that I was too gentle with the female staff who were mothers. In fact, I was always saddened and bringing up the issue of having women on the cash registers when their children were left at school out of regular school hours just because we didn't do a rota with sufficient staff to cover the daily shifts. I got fed up of seeing grown women cry and my hands being tied, so in a sense, I really didn't fit into the culture of this organisation. Many nights I would go home and my conscience would bother me about some of the things our employees endured.

Even though my life had just taken the proverbial leap off the edge of a cliff, my dependents and family remained just as strongly reliant on me. I didn't know whether to cry or laugh when I received a letter from a friend back in Jamaica a few days after my sacking, who was asking me to give her an update on how I was coming along in collecting money to cover her university tuition and fees. I knew in my heart that I could do nothing for her, and it pained me to think

Ava Brown

about how this would be yet another person I loved who I would be letting down. I would have rather just crumpled up the letter, thrown my phone into the river, and pretended like the request had never existed, but I couldn't do that.

I sat down and put pen to paper:

My dearest Cassie,

I write to you this morning in one of the lowest states I have ever found myself in; my life just seems to be a series of low points. I am beginning to wonder if I have personality disorder or something wrong with me that attracts this kind of oppression. I am depressed beyond anything I have ever felt before; I don't even have the words to properly express what I am going through. When I am not numb, I am having a panic attack, and I feel like I am very near not being able to cope.

Just the hustle of trying to stay on top of the most basic bills makes me miserable. Being on my own and with no one to help emotionally or financially is killing me.

Simply put, I am tired of life. I sit here typing and crying...and thinking how very tired I am of fighting this unwinnable battle that is my life. I want out of this rat race. If it weren't for Jasmin I would probably be searching for a way to exit this life entirely, but I cannot pass my sorrow or burden on to her.

I love her more than life itself. I have to hang on for her. But, all she sees of me is the depression, which makes me impatient, short-tempered, insecure and frustrated to distraction.

It was very hard for me to sit down and write this to you. I hate having to admit how much my life has regressed. I am so unhappy here in London and I want desperately to return to my native Jamaica. However, Jasmin is now going ten and she doesn't want to leave;

237

London is almost all she knows and her dad lives here. All of the jobs I have found here have been jobs of circumstance and nothing I would have chosen. The hours have prevented me from even being a mum properly.

I just received word that my mortgage has gone up due to the credit crunch. I had no idea how to pay it now that I am out of the job at the grocery store, but now to think that it is even higher than I expected, I really don't see how this will work out. I finally made an appointment to see a physiologist and she agreed that I need to be under some attentive care, but where will I find the money to cover such an additional expense? I am nearing a break-down.

"How low can one get tossed before they just sink into nothingness?"

CHAPTER 22

"I think men become who we want them to be. They curve into the man that we expect them to be and when we are no longer there, they become who they really are."

The day that I lost my job, my house seemed lonelier than it had ever felt before. I sat alone in my room and cried. As I cradled my pillow for comfort, I remembered how so many times before Tobore would have been the one snuggling next to me in bed, holding me while I wept into his shoulder, assuring me that however bleak the situation was, he would help see me through it. It broke my heart even more to think that I had lost that companionship, to know that I was really on my own against the world now.

Just days before, I had contemplated requesting that Tobore sign off his part of our house in Jamaica, so that it would be under my name solely. This would allow me to cut off my last tie to the one person who should have been my partner for life. Now, here I was with the weight of the world pressing even harder on my shoulders. I tried in vain to pull myself out of the emotional black hole that was consuming me, and even sleep proved to be another luxury denied to me. I started using sleeping pills, but the few hours of pharmaceutically-induced unconsciousness never left me feeling refreshed.

Before the sacking, I had been looking for other jobs, I had even gotten a few interviews (which I had secretly attended so as not to jeopardise my already tenuous position). My efforts had been rather weak and unsuccessful though, largely because of the extensive time demands from the store and my distraction with all the other pressures in my personal life. Now, I was living in a constant state of needling anxiety and on the verge of completely losing my ability to function in even the simplest of daily tasks. When I would sit down to try to take stock of my situation to come up with a productive plan, I would start to feel the walls closing in on me and the air becoming thick and hard to breathe in. There was nothing that I wanted more than to run outside and escape everything that was constraining me.

I knew I couldn't go on like this, so I asked my general practitioner for a referral to a psychologist. Having a stranger to talk too seemed more effective at that time than leaning on my friends alone. They had their own issues, and I also didn't know who could handle the terrors in my past that I was still carrying around. I did consider calling on Tobore at this time, to make him my confidante, after all, we were on friendly terms with one another and he already knew all of my past. Our wedding anniversary was coming up and he had even called to ask if he could take me out for a private dinner that night. I had agreed because I was fairly certain there would be no expectations that we would have of one another.

We had built a comfortable platonic relationship and it benefited Jasmin as much as it did Tobore and I. Gone were the days of angry glaring across the table and screaming matches over the smallest of offences. We were able to do things together, as a family in peace, like taking trips to animal parks and sharing holiday dinners. Tobore and I still supported each other financially too. If he was ever in a bind, he knew he could come to me to borrow cash and I knew I could count on him for the same; unfortunately, neither of us had much to spare at any time since coming to the UK.

I found out that the wait to get a psychologist appointment was months, so I decided to reach out to

Tobore for some emotional support. Over the next weeks and months, I felt us really connecting in a meaningful way and thought maybe it was because we were building a friendship without the distraction of romantic involvement. We had even had several conversations where I shared with him my desire to find a man to share that physical side of life with, discussing my hopes for the occasional man I found attractive or who things could turn intimate with. Little did I know, this was piercing his heart.

Tobore's silent torment finally came to my attention when something began to develop between him and a single parent from Jasmin's school. He began acting very strange and unnecessarily hostile around me, so I confronted him about it; I was not expecting what he told me next. He said that he still loved me with the same depth as when we conceived our daughter, and told me that he couldn't ever love anyone else like this. He even told me that I was the only person he would ever consider having another child with, and expressed the deepest regret for how far we had strayed from one another and all of the things that had happened in the years we had been apart.

My heart melted. I began to think that somehow, after all that we had gone through as a couple, we were both subconsciously involved and had been all along. Maybe, I wondered, nothing had worked out with other people because neither of us had ever really wanted to move on. We hadn't been intimate in a very long time, and the thought of it scared me in a way. I had come to love and treasure our friendship and I wasn't completely sure how I felt about abandoning that to enter into the tumult that we had left behind when we left each other's beds. The one thing I was sure of though was that at this time in my life, I could not emotionally or mentally handle one more complication.

I feared that this chance at reconciliation might have to be delayed.

I had started making applications for work again, but nothing was panning out. One afternoon, after a particularly dismal interview, I was driving home and feeling so low that I was thinking how much better life would be if someone would just run a light so that I could be met by angels who would carry me off to heaven. This was an insane thought, I knew, so I called Tobore and immediately started crying so hard that I could barely talk. He told me to pull off the road and compose myself, then to head straight home. He would be there shortly. I did so, taking only a few minutes to get my emotions under control and reaching the house only about five minutes later. As soon as I arrived, I sat down to wait for Tobore and Kem and I fell into conversation about my low mood. She offered to make me something to eat, but I declined because Tobore would be arriving any moment and I wasn't hungry.

Before I knew it, two hours had elapsed. Tobore finally arrived, but he seemed in such a normal mood that I figured he had just been waylaid by something unimportant. He took me for a drive and we talked. He listened to all of my complaints and fears and gave all of the right bolstering responses. By the time he dropped me off at home, I felt ready to go on with my life's battle. I was even able to make a few more appointments for potential job leads, one of which they told me to come in for right away. I grabbed my purse and was heading out the door when a call came from Jasmin's school. They needed me to bring her asthma medication because she was in the nurse's office with some worrying symptoms.

I cursed my luck. If I went, I would miss the meeting with the employment agency, but my child's health was much too important to be put second to anything else. I decided to call Tobore and ask him to help out once more today. Because he had just been so solicitous towards me, I was a bit surprised by his reticence to help out with this small situation, but there really was no time to dilly-dally. I told him that I would take care of it myself and not to worry.

I jumped in my car and drove to the school to drop off the medication. I called the employment agency and asked if I could be a few minutes late, but was told that their schedule wouldn't accommodate the delay. So, I drove home. Kem told me that Tobore had been at the house just a few minutes before I came back, but he had left when she told him I had already gone to make the delivery. Something in her voice made me nervous and I asked her what she was holding back. She told me that he had come to the front door alone, but that she had seen someone else waiting for him in the car, a woman.

I rolled my eyes dismissively and told her that it was probably just some friend that needed a favour that day like I did. Her silence let me know that I was being a fool. She told me that it was clearly something else. The woman was very young and dressed like she was ready for a hot date, looking bored and very at-home in the front passenger seat with her feet propped up on the dashboard. She didn't need to say anything more about what she had seen; my heart recognised the truth of the matter.

I called Tobore to ask him about who the girl was that he was spending his day off with. He immediately went on the defensive and said it was none of my business. I told him that since he had just professed his undying love to me and opened the door to our reconciliation, it was most certainly my business. His tone turned very gruff and harsh, and he said that I was jumping to conclusions in my head about what he wanted of me. He said that our friendship was the end of whatever would be between us and that was where our relationship was and that was where it ended. I felt tricked and utterly betrayed. In an instant, all of the trust and love that I felt for him disappeared with a finality that would affect the rest of our lives.

I knew that we would still have to interact with each other as Jasmin's parents, but I closed my heart to him beyond anything else. A week later, as I was continuing my job hunt around town, I got a call from Kem saying that Jasmin had been sent home from school with worsening symptoms and she needed to get to a doctor right away. I was half way across town and knew I couldn't get back home through traffic within the next hour. I moved my heart into a professional mode, thinking that I would call Tobore as Jasmin's father to come and assist with his child getting to the hospital since it was again his day off. He agreed and drove straight to my home, but quickly announced to Kem that he thought she looked fine. In his opinion, she didn't need a doctor. He said that there was nothing wrong with her that a nap wouldn't fix.

I found out later that he really was just anxious to get back to his girlfriend and had gone home grousing to a mutual friend that a visit to doctor would have taken hours out of his day, just to possibly find out that she had a typical virus or something else common in kids. Back at home, though, Jasmin rapidly grew worse and Kem became so frightened that she had me call another friend who came over and immediately drove Jasmin to the closest hospital. Jasmin's state upon arrival was so alarming that she was admitted and prepped for surgery to address acute appendicitis.

The news shook me to my core. My baby was so sick that she needed to be cut open? My shock quickly switched to a seething anger towards Tobore. How dare he be so flippant about our child's health, no matter what the reason. The doctor had told me on the phone that appendicitis could be deadly if left untreated; she could have died if we had ignored her symptoms. If I had known then the real reason why he left (to covert with his new paramour) I don't know what I would have done. I rushed to the hospital and found Tobore there at her bedside. My anger with him had only grown during the drive and I flew into a rage at the sight of him. I literally chased him out of the room, screaming all sorts of accusations that he may have caused her death by his ignorant attitude.

I settled into the chair next to Jasmin's bed and refused to leave her for the night, even though the nurses advised me that visiting hours had ended. At around three am, a nurse came around to check in. I told her that Jasmin had kept telling me that her IV was hurting her, saying "Mummy, this isn't comfy" while trying to pull on it. I asked the nurse to check it, and it's a good thing I did because she discovered that the cannula wasn't placed correctly. She said that they would try to re-place it right away, but I stopped her and asked why she needed it. She said it was all part of the precaution to have her ready if they found out that she had appendicitis and if they needed to operate on her.

I was confused, from what I understood Jasmin had already been diagnosed. I asked the nurse to clarify everything and she said that they really didn't know what was wrong with my baby. They just suspected appendicitis, but the tests had all been inconclusive. I did not know very much about medicine or diseases, such as appendicitis, but I was appalled that they were getting my daughter ready for surgery without really knowing what was wrong with her, or what they needed to do. Surgery was so invasive and such a physical trauma. I didn't want her subjected to it on a suspicion. I demanded that they do more testing and get a better handle on what was really wrong. In the end, the nurse called the doctor and they acquiesced to me, and before noon, all of Jasmin's symptoms had resolved and she was released from the hospital; the test results came back and ruled out appendicitis.

Over the next few weeks, Tobore's visits were very infrequent. Jasmin noticed and started complaining that he was neglecting her, so I doubled my efforts to keep them in contact in other ways. They would still get together on the weekends, only now he would just drop in for the minute it took to collect her and her things before they sped off in the car. Each time she came back from these visits, she would tell me about a girl that would stay with them for the whole weekend. I could tell she was jealous of the attention he would shower on this woman; seeing it as time stolen away from her. Tobore was blind to this, though. Jasmin was even demoted to the back seat of the car on journeys, even though it was an unspoken rule that this is where she would sit in both of our cars. But the front seat was now occupied by Tobore's latest woman.

It all came to a head a short time later, when one afternoon I found Jasmin crying in the bedroom. She said that her daddy never paid attention to her anymore. It broke my heart to see her suffering like this, so I called Tobore to ask him to talk to her and to get his act together for her sake. He immediately flew into me, telling me that his personal life and his relationship with his daughter were none of my business. But, as every mother knows, anything that affects your child immediately becomes your business. I gave him a stern dressing down and he agreed to speak to her about it.

I was afraid that Jasmin would get on the phone and crumble into a frail little girl that gave up fighting for

Ava Brown

herself, but I was filled with pride when she got on the phone and told him everything she had just told me. She asked him when she could see him next and they settled on that Wednesday when his next day off was. I drove her to his house on the appointed day, but asked her to first wait in the car while I had a quick talk with him. My intent was to stress to him the seriousness of the situation and that he couldn't merely dismiss her upset. However, what happened next changed my life forever.

"Totally broken and fragile can scare you forever if you let it."

CHAPTER 23

"Letting go is sometimes hard, but a necessity in an effort to grow."

Tobore answered the door and silently invited me inside with a wave of his hand. We started talking about the situation, and he immediately became furious, yelling at me that I cannot control his life. The personal attack took me off guard, but I got some clarity when he told he thought my problem was that I didn't want him, but I didn't want him to be with anyone else. The conversation became an all-out argument, in each other faces and screaming at the tops of our lungs. He was angrier than I had ever seen him before.

His eyes turned bloodshot red, and before I knew it he lunged forward and grabbed me by the throat, squeezing so hard I chocked for breath. I managed to bite his other hand so hard that he dropped his grasp on me, but before I could recover my wits, he had pushed me into the kitchen and we were both striking at each other. I saw his fist coming hard at me, and I grabbed a knife off the counter. I don't know what I was planning to do with it, but it didn't matter because he had already shoved me into the passage and slapped me across the face. I had dropped the knife in the melee and in defence, kicked him hard in the leg. I sensed a hot wetness on my face and reached up to touch, only to realise I was gushing blood from somewhere. I was filled with terror and looked at Tobore, only to see that he was bleeding too.

For some reason, this realisation set a fire in me. I reared back to fly at him with all my force, but he had grabbed a broom and used it to strike me across the face. The pain was tremendous and nothing like I had ever felt before. I was sure he had broken my nose and

I found myself flat on the floor. He was standing over me, screaming and cursing that I had rejected him and that it was his time to take out his revenge on me once and for all. I will never forget the coldness in his voice when he said he had been waiting for this moment since before we left Jamaica. He said I had brought this on myself because I had cheated on him and made him look like a fool.

I was in total shock. A strange silence fell between us and he finally grabbed me and pulled me up roughly, turning and shutting himself in a side room. I didn't know what to do. The whole scene felt like I had just experienced a nightmare and was merely waking from it. I started to come to my senses quickly, and remembered that Jasmin was still sitting outside waiting in the car. I grabbed at a curtain on the front window and wiped the blood from my face, thinking that I could simply walk out and pretend that nothing had happened. I didn't realise that I was covered in blood. As soon as Jasmin saw me, her eyes widened in shock and she started crying.

I tried to calm her down and told her that I was going to be ok, but that I needed to call the police. She begged me not to, saying that she didn't want her dad to get into trouble. What was I to do? She was in hysterics at the thought of losing him. I started the car up and drove home. I finally got Jasmin to calm down by saying that adults, especially parents, sometimes have disagreements and it was nothing for her to worry about. I began to try to figure out how to handle the situation. I decided to call Tobore's newest female friend, who had been spending a lot of time at his house. I had heard that she was a mother also, and I thought that maybe I could explain to her what I tried to explain to Tobore about Jasmin's being upset with him not spending enough quality time with her. My irrational hope was that she would pass on the message I had originally intended to get across before our altercation.

I meant to only ask her to try to help Tobore understand how Jasmin was feeling and ask that she help him be a bit more sensible and conscious of his daughter's feelings. I ignorantly assumed that as a female and a mother, she would be my ally and she would understand that girls are far more wanting of their dad's attention. After all, I was still legally married to him and I also hoped she would respect that. I immediately found out how foolish I was being. As soon as I said hello and introduced myself, she laid into me. "Ey dutty gal, a long time me a wait pon you fi call me! Why the fuck you nuh left him alone and divorce him so him can be free to love who him want? Why the fuck you nuh get it that you and him over? Why you keep calling him to come round to you fucking yard? You nuh get it you a wife pon paper, but mi a him baby mother! Fuck off, gal, I am pregnant with his son. The one you could never give him."

I couldn't even speak. Instead, I just hung up the phone. Her words hurt me more than any of the blows that Tobore had rained down on me earlier that day. Clearly, she had been fed the idea that I was the one holding onto him, when in fact it was he who was holding on to me. Mainly because divorce would have ruined his chances to get his citizenship in the UK. The pregnancy also pierced me and I understood why it did. To some extent, during one of our last civil conversations just a few weeks before, Tobore and I had decided that if we were still estranged, and not with anyone else (especially me) by the time I turned 35, we would come together and have a baby so that Jasmin would have a full sibling.

The conversation with this woman was not over yet though. She must have used my phone number off the caller ID to start sending me abusive text messages, threatening my life and calling me all sorts of despicable names. I began to put two and two together, remembering her from an earlier time with Tobore and how he had vehemently denied having any interest in her, saying that she was just some 'ghetto gal' from his work. I should have just turned off my phone, but I was so incensed at the whole situation that I fell into a text battle with this person who I didn't even know. I had no one to blame but myself for this event. Even though my intentions for contacting her had been good, I had opened the floodgates to set us on this hateful path.

I went outside to talk to my friend Norma on the phone and to try to calm down. She tried to encourage me to delete the hateful texts, but I felt that I needed to keep them as evidence if things deteriorated further. The intensity of the situation exhausted me. I collapsed into a heap on the ground and buried my head in my hands. Just then, I heard a car stop and heavy footsteps come up the walkway. I lifted my head only slightly to see who was visiting me at this inopportune time and was confused to see three sets of shining black shoes. I lifted my head slowly up the legs of three sturdy police officers, their hands firmly on their truncheons. I instantly knew that they were here for me. Tobore must have called them to report me after I had left his house.

One of the officers calmly asked if I was Ava Brown and I told them yes. They beckoned me to get up off the ground and said that they needed me to come with them. I wasn't about to object. I cursed myself for not having called the police first and instead giving in to my young daughter's wishes of not wanting to cause Tobore any more trouble than we already had in our lives as immigrants. I told the men that I would come quietly and they allowed me to first tell my sister that I would be out so that she could watch my daughter. If Jasmin asked where I was going, my plan was to tell her that I was just going out for a walk to clear my head. However, Jasmin is the one who met me at the door, and I saw the extreme anguish on her face as she noticed the police standing in the background.

Before anything else could happen, Jasmin began screaming and flailing, her heart tormented. She banged her head hard on the wall and fell. The police came rushing forth to help with the situation and when they persuaded her to take deep breaths she calmed down to a miserable crying state. They tried to explain to her that they just wanted to take her mum somewhere quiet for a while so that we could have a talk, but my child was far too intelligent and she knew better. In the end, I left with them, sitting like a scolded child in the back of the police car. Luckily, they spared me the handcuffs because I was being cooperative. My whole being was in shock, I couldn't even feel my heart beating and thought that maybe I had died and my spirit was just somehow locked inside my body. I spoke up to make sure of the reality of the situation. I asked if I could use my phone to make a call. That was when they gave me the official word that I was under arrest; they then confiscated my phone and they read me my rights.

We arrived at a police station in Norwood, driven up a back entrance and straight to where the cells were. I had remained silent for the entire drive, but my mind was working overtime. I kept asking myself how someone who had once loved me so intensely, someone who had shared so many momentous events in my life, someone who relied on me as much as I did on him could have done this to me. I was crying copiously and could hardly understand what was being said to me when the booking process had begun. I finally heard the charge against me; Tobore had reported that I had come to his house and instigated a physical attack. I finally found my voice and tried to tell the police that they had it all wrong, but they were quite dismissive at this stage and said that they were just doing their jobs.

I realised that I had no advocate in this police station, so I decided that my best tact was just to stay quiet. My god I was shaking with fear! In no time, I was being led further into the building. Someone removed my belt and took off all of my jewellery. A body search was then performed by a female officer, and in the background, I could hear another officer making account of my possessions. Finally, I was given one phone call, which I used to call home and talk to Jasmin to continue to reassure her that I would be fine and home soon.

After the call, I was taken to be fingerprinted, to give a DNA sample (by mouth swab) taken and to have my mug shot taken. Everything they did was so invasive, on a physical and a spiritual level. I knew I was experiencing what it was like to lose my freedom, and I flashed back to how awful the experience must have been for my little sister in those weeks before her death. The jail staff asked if I needed anything and I requested to see a doctor and a solicitor. I still had open wounds from the earlier altercation with Tobore and I was afraid of infection or scaring if they were not attended to. They said that it was all in process and ushered me down to a cell.

When I heard the heavy metal lock clank into place, I felt lower than I ever had in my entire life. The whole situation was surreal, almost as if I was suddenly in a TV show. Again, I started to think that maybe I was simply experiencing a very lucid stress nightmare on the eve before I was to confront Tobore about spending more one-on-one time with our daughter. Maybe I had fallen out of bed and was lying on the hard floor of my house; that must be the uncomfortable feeling under my back. But, no, it was really the hard bed in the cold cell I was occupying. I had to face the reality that I was in jail, placed there under the false accusations made by husband. It was clear that he was at war with me, and I was losing the battle.

I started reflecting on our relationship from a more realistic perspective. One in which my heart was closed off and deadened to him. I realised how many mistakes I had made with him, especially in re-trusting him after the first episode of him creating a child with another woman and me still allowing him to move to London with us. How foolish I had been to think that we could ever make anything out of the deteriorated shell of a marriage we had. I was shocked at how much he had changed as a person from the man I believed he was in those blissful first years we spend as a young couple while I was in teaching college. How could that loving young man be the same person who just sent the police to arrest me by using a blatant lie?

Even more troubling was the thought of how this man, who had changed so drastically, could still be a loving and cautious father with Jasmin? Did he not think at all about how this false accusation against me would affect her emotional well-being and her livelihood? I remembered the status of my citizenship right then, and my body went numb again. How would an arrest affect that? And, if my application was negatively affected, both his and Jasmin's would be in jeopardy as well. How could he have not thought about that?

I supposed he had reached a point where he just didn't care about any of it anymore. Something must have given him enough confidence in his own chances to feel like he could get citizenship without me. I realised that, finally, he must really see the end of us. There was no going back from this event, our lives even as parents to a shared child were separated from one another from that moment on.

I didn't know what else to do. I was absolutely powerless to the forces shaping my life around me. I closed my eyes and asked God to just give me the courage and strength to get out of the entire mess that my life had become since coming to London. I asked God to work a miracle so that I would somehow get released before the night fell. That way, I could be home before Jasmin fell asleep and I could ease her fears. I laid there crying for who knows how long. I cried until my eyes hurt and there were no more tears to come out of them. Each time the jailers passed by for a routine inspection, I would ask if my doctor or lawyer had arrived to see me yet. Each time they told me no.

On the fourth pass, they asked if I wanted anything to eat. I had been so consumed with distraught that the thought of food had never crossed my mind, even though I hadn't eaten since before eight o'clock that morning and it was now late afternoon. I merely mumbled that I wasn't hungry. There was a toilet in the cell, and although I wanted to pee, I just couldn't make myself use it as the cell was open for all to see. I had been in the cell for around four hours when the doctor finally arrived. He made some sort of joke about the delay being caused by 'London's Sunday service'. I suppose this was his attempt to lighten my heavy mood, but it didn't work. His visit afforded me some freedom since I was taken out of my cell for the examination and treatment.

I stupidly thought that this was my chance to finally be absolved of the false accusations. Certainly, this doctor would see that I was beaten up and call for my release. Instead, he simply went over me from head to toe, taking blood samples from the still open gashes on my lip and in my mouth, and made a report that confirmed that I was had been badly beaten up. I remember him even noting the slap marks on my face, where the impact of Tobore's hand had broken the blood vessels under my skin. After this, he left and I was taken promptly back to my cell.

I began to have all kinds of panicked thoughts. What if I was never released? What if this was my new home? What if social services took Jasmin away because I was an unfit mother locked up in jail? The lady who I had made hurried arrangements with to watch her because Kem had had to leave couldn't stay there overnight. What would happen to my child then? Would she just be left at home alone?

I stared at the walls of the cell, and no answers came to my fearful questions. The ceiling and walls were covered with the names of all who 'WUZ ERE', scratched into the plaster by countless hands. I had no interest in proudly claiming my residence in this jail. Soon, though, I received word that my appointed lawyer had arrived and I was escorted to the room where he and I were allowed to talk. I told him the truth of what had happened at Tobore's; leaving out no detail, not even the ones that made me look bad. He made non-committal responses to all of my statements. Afterwards, I was taken to meet with another set of police officers in yet another room, where they had tape recording equipment and they made official record of my statement.

The lawyer had accompanied me to make my statement, and I'm glad he did because it was clear from the first moment that the police thought I was lying. They tried to convince the lawyer that I was guilty, but he stood his ground defending me and continued to ask for proof of the accusations against me. After an interminable back-and-forth, the policewoman agreed with the lawyer and said that the information just wasn't strong enough to prove that Tobore was telling the truth in his accusation against me. Instead of being released immediately, I was placed back into my cell while they processed all the paperwork and made records in their database of the event, my statements and all of my very personal information. I was finally released, with the knowledge that my fingerprints and DNA would be on file for six years before being deleted. I couldn't believe it; I was now in the police database all thanks to my husband.

As I was gathering my belongings, the last policewoman who had been present for the debate with my lawyer came over and gave me a pep talk. She told me that I was lucky to be going home and reminded me that I needed to put everything with Tobore behind me and just focus on my child. She had a warm, almost motherly, tone of voice when she told me to leave this man out of my life, saying he didn't mean me any good and I would be fighting a losing battle with him. She even told me that I had the right to go downstairs and make a report against him, based on the evidence of my bodily harm that was clear for all to see. But, without saying anything we both knew this would only be stirring the hornet's nest. Besides, I was still struggling with the immense guilt of the damage I would cause to him by doing so. Even though he had just done this horrible thing to me, I could not find it within myself to do it back to him.

At this stage, I knew that I needed to go home to be with my child. I had no money, it was late and I still needed to find a way home. I wasn't about to dawdle at the station. What if they changed their minds and tried to re-arrest me? I almost ran outside to the high street and frantically waived down a cab. On my way to the house, I called my friend who was still sitting for Jasmin to ask if she had money on her. She said yes and I breathed a sigh of relief, something was finally going my way. When I got home, all I could do was grab Jasmin and hug her so tight like I was never going to let her go. We were both crying and clinging onto each other for quite some time.

My friend who had come to watch her told me that after I had been picked up by the police, Tobore's brother had arrived and said that he was there to pick Jasmin up to stay with her father. Since I had told her the situation (and Jasmin had already told her of her own fright after seeing my substantial physical injuries), she knew better than to believe this ruse. There was no way she was going to give Jasmin to anyone in my absence. I thanked her profusely and she headed home to her own waiting family. Jasmin fell asleep quickly; she was so exhausted after the stress of the day. I tossed and turned with fitful nightmares about the police coming back to get me again.

Our lives were never the same after that day. It was another cruel reminder in my life that everything you know can be taken away in a moment; how your life's path can be changed drastically without your intent or input. The woman who was currently carrying Tobore's third child started a campaign of hate against me - emails, letters, and phone calls. I was constantly bombarded, but my experience with being arrested on false charges had frightened me so much that I could not trust the police to help me with this situation. I was so traumatised by all of the events that I was unable to focus on the fact that I wasn't working and no money was coming in.

My friends in London rallied around me and Jasmin during this time and provided what little comfort and money they could to help us. Since Jasmin's birthday was coming up, my friend Norma invited us to her house for the celebration. Jasmin agreed to the plan right away because she had decided on her own that she didn't want to see her father anymore. I finally felt free to file for divorce; there was nothing left tying us together. As soon as I was legally classified as a single mother, I qualified for social assistance and it provided such a positive change in my life that I had never anticipated.

The first thing I needed to do was get myself back together emotionally, and truthfully, this was one of the hardest things I had ever done. The experience of being arrested and locked up had affected my self-esteem in ways that I had never imagined. I felt like society had labelled me as a criminal and I lost the confidence in who I was. I no longer saw myself as an independent tenacious woman, but as a shameful blotch on society. This went against everything at my core. I knew that if I was to survive and be an effective mother for Jasmin, I would have to get back to who I was before this unfair event took place.

Accepting that Tobore was not the man I thought he was proved to be just as hard. I relied heavily on my faith during this time, and began to see God's hand in many of the events of the past years. In a way, He had continually showed me that this was not the relationship for me - for either of us - but I had been too strong-headed to recognise it. Serving the divorce papers to Tobore was yet another challenge. He had moved residences and I could not get anyone to divulge his location. All I found out was that he had moved in with the woman carrying his child and her family.

I finally discovered his whereabouts when one of my friends saw the two of them shopping at a grocery store nearby my house. I was shocked to find out that they lived relatively close to Jasmin and me, yet he had never once reached out to her since that fateful day. I was more heartbroken to learn that he was doing very well, both personally and financially. My friend said that he and the woman were laughing and joking like young lovers through the store, with a whole trolley full of items. Meanwhile, Jasmin and I were wondering where our next meal was going to come from since I had no money, we were hungry and our cupboards were empty.

I went back to the same traumatised and fearful state that I had fallen into after the attack in Jamaica that had precipitated our move to London. Every time I heard a police car, I became nervous and agitated, thinking that Tobore was again exerting his revenge on me. Kem and her daughter were still living with us, but she was so displeased with the situation of me being jobless and anxious, that she had decided to return to Jamaica. Instead of being relieved that I would have two less people to be responsible for, I was heartsick that I would be losing the little in-house support system I had.

Our situation only became more challenging over the next weeks. Tobore finally reached out to start seeing Jasmin again, but he refused to let her go to his home or to see her inside of mine. Instead, he proposed that I bring her to meet him on the street in a neutral area where he would park his car and they could spend a few minutes talking. I felt like this was too disrespectful to our daughter and I turned down his offer. I told him that we needed to find a more suitable environment than a car on the side of the road for them to rebuild their father-daughter relationship.

He responded by sending a letter through his solicitor that demanded visitation with Jasmin under any condition, and accusing me of unlawful denial of contact with his child. Besides this stress, I had started falling behind on my mortgage payments and I was now at risk of losing our home. Something had to change in our lives and soon. I had a long, serious talk with Jasmin about our situation. I suggested that we may be in a better position if we were to quit London and go back to Jamaica for a while. Even though it broke my heart, I told her she had the option of staying in London with her dad, if she really wanted to. My sweet girl spared not one moment in declining the offer and saying that she wanted to come along with me no matter where we went.

I started planning for our move home. I put our house on the market, but quickly realised that we would fare better finding renters. I have to admit that there was a huge relief in preparing to go back to Jamaica. I had wanted out of London for a long time now, but I had always consulted Tobore on it before. His response was always to dissuade me, telling me I would mess up our immigration status and ruin everything I had worked so hard for already. Now, without him, the decision was completely up to me. I knew that my situation was so dire at the moment that if I stayed in London, I would lose my house, and my sanity.

As the day neared for us to return back to the homeland, I assaulted myself with blame for the mess that had led all of us to this moment in time. I blamed myself for bringing Tobore to London; I blamed myself for the deterioration of Jasmin and Tobore's relationship and for all the hardships that we had endured as immigrants in this harsh new country. I convinced myself that I was a complete failure in all aspects of my life; as a wife, as a mother, and as a career woman. It was in this fog of self-hate and depression that I booked our flights back to Jamaica and led my child back home to the land of her ancestors in hope of re-joining the well-worn path that they had forged from the slave ships to independence. After all, we were both born of their spirit of tenacity and resilience, and our path still had many steps to go.

"Life and revenge can be a very messy affair."

Press Non Fiction Footnotes

An interview with Ava Brown

What was the inspiration to write Bamboo& Fern?
I was going through a difficult patch and felt overwhelmed, so putting my feelings on paper was cathartic. It just developed from there.

What book are you reading at the moment?
Maya Angelo's 'Why the cage bird sing'.

Do you have a favourite time of day when you finding writing easiest?
Yes, I write at nights it's so quiet. The world is asleep and my keyboard talks to me.

Is there a favourite place to write?
My dining room table as to be honest, it's near to the larder.

What fictional character would you like to be?
A genie so I could grant myself my ultimate wish.

Who would you say the greatest writer is?
Nancy Rosenberg Taylor and John Grisham

Apart from writing what other jobs have you done?
I am a mum and a wife as well as someone who has done many roles from retail management, teaching, sales, banking and account management.

What are you working on at the moment?
I am working on my project 'Ava's Kitchen' - A Life Coach and Family Food Therapist Project as well as my second book 'Walk on Through Your Dreams' - the

second part of my autobiography. This is where the happy bits come in somehow.

Ava Brown

Contact Me

If you have been inspired by my story and would like to know more about how I can help you, I would love to hear from you. You can contact me directly via any of the following methods:

www.avabrown.org

www.bambooandfern.com

Twitter @avabrown24

Facebook is Av Brown
https://www.facebook.com/#!/ava.brown.10048

https:// www. facebook.com/ pages/ Bamboo-Fern/ 1434190263522565

https://www.linkedin.com/profile/view?id=30310633& trk=nav_responsive_tab_profile

Email: info@avabrown.org info and marketing and enquruies@bambooandfern.com

Quotes by Ava Brown

Over the years life has inspired me to write these quotes, they have normally come out of an experience. I enjoyed writing them as well as using them and even applying them and I hope you do too.

"Birth is a special time for any mother; she forgets all her struggles and latches unto the bundle of joy she is gifted with."

"Even without recognition, in the coldest part of us, fear has burnt from conception".

"True identity for some, at times is hard to recognize leading to questioning of characters and traits, for some even leads to questions about one's existence".

"Our entry into the world is most met with laughter and tears of joy; do we cry as we are fearful or hopeful?"

"Far too often we hide behind that which makes us comfortable, looking for a shelter from the truth of our pain and sadness as they are too difficult and devastating to confront".

"What makes us ultimately happy is sometimes disguised in shadows of turmoil."

"Hidden happiness awaits if we stop to see beyond the now, only that is most times almost impossible."

"They say nothing worth having comes easily, Yet we could benefit from balls thrown at us that weren't always curved."

Ava Brown

"Sometimes we go through life feeling broken and something magical happens to change that; like the birth of an innocent life."

"Sometimes our lives have to be turned upside down and rebuilt in an effort to take us to the God given place we are meant to be".

"I have realised that we can directly measure life by our will to endure, persevere and survive".

"Watered baptism is said to be the only thing to cleanse original sin, thus sins are stained and embedded in us. However, forgiveness is saved for the contrite making it hard to erase the embedded evil."

"I've learnt to let my instincts and gut guide me in all I do, regardless of how things seem. "

"Sometimes it's best to be unsure of what lies ahead of us because if we knew, there wouldn't be any great adventure or ability or build resilience."

"The unknown is sometimes started with excitement and anticipation that isn't realise at firs. It's then that we have to accept we weren't prepared for the unknown."

"Being in the wilderness without a familiar object is like being left to die, but faith will allow you to survive until rescue can come."

"The mundane things in modern life, like technology, can be one's best friend in the desert."

Bamboo & Fern

"Life can sometimes toss, shove and send you into the wilderness before it brings you back to civilization, the place you ideally want to be at."

"The presence, support and comfort of family is the best remedy for the soul."

"Readjustments can sometimes feel like a crisis on self-esteem."

"Perseverance can be the platform on which goodness is staged."

"The most significant weapon people can use against us is playing with our minds."

"Ego can ignite a satisfaction so deep within us, regardless of the consequences."

"Money is a prison for those less fortunate to have been born without it."

"When all around you seems to be a whirlwind, just stand still and allow the calm to take effect around you. It will sort out the chaos".

"Societies differ and can make or break you, so you must be mindful to stay unbroken as those same societies will eject you if you are weakened."

"Struggles can be medicinal."

"While trying to carve out your own destiny, you sometimes leave dents in someone else's."

"Death is a thief, it robs us of our loved ones and keeps a hold of all the person is and was."

"Some events in life can rob you of your soul, but our bodies function nonetheless."

"Being a mother shouldn't just apply to your biological child, but should transcend to each child you come into contact with."

"Someone else's errors can be the penalty of the innocent."

"Heartbreaks are not always caused by people or intimate love gone wrong; they can come in unexpected forms, and I have had my fair share of all types."

"Sometimes, just swimming into the waves is all you can do, letting the tide carry you to the destined place."

"The unknown is wrapped in cycles of belief and dare-to."

"Reputations can attach themselves to us and become a permanent part of our person."

"Exit strategies can creep upon us so unknowingly."

"Removing one brick from a stack can send walls crumbling down. Quickly escaping isn't always possible so we sometimes get crushed."

"How low can one get tossed before they just sink into nothingness?"

"I think men become who we want them to be. They curve into the man that we expect them to be and when

we are no longer there, they become who they really are."

"Totally broken and fragile can scare you forever if you let it."

"Letting go is sometimes hard, but a necessity in an effort to grow."

Ava Brown

CPSIA information can be obtained
at www.ICGtesting.com
Printed in the USA
BVHW020554260421
605848BV00014B/840

9 780993 144295